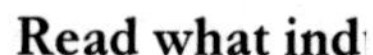

Read what ind 

n.

"Finally - a book that tackles the unique challenges of the high-tech capital equipment industry. Mike has packed into one book the strategies, tactics, and tools that could take a lifetime to develop on your own. *Equipped to Win* is a must-read for anyone charged with high-tech capital equipment strategy, product management, or marketing."

- John Peeler, Chief Executive Officer, Veeco Instruments, Inc.

"Companies in these markets regularly bet their futures on new product and platform introductions. The stakes couldn't be higher. In *Equipped to Win*, Mike provides practical advice and tools to help executives and product marketing managers navigate key issues and produce winning results."

- David Gray, Ph.D., Vice President of Strategic Development, GT Solar International, Inc.

"*Equipped to Win* is not only a great primer for young equipment company entrepreneurs, but it is also a solid reference for seasoned executives as they set out to create competitive advantage and grow their companies."

- Pete Simone, Retired Chief Executive Officer and current Director of several public high-technology equipment companies

"In *Equipped to Win*, Mike has captured the strategies and tactics that have made him successful in the capital equipment business. This book should be required reading for everyone from executives to engineering, product, and sales managers."

- Don Kania, Ph.D., President and Chief Executive Officer, FEI Company

"In *Equipped to Win,* Michael addresses the key elements and common pitfalls of capital equipment marketing and has tied them together in a comprehensive guide. This is not a 'blot out the sun' book on marketing theory; *Equipped to Win* is a truly useful day-to-day management tool for any high-tech capital equipment supplier."

- John Aldeborgh, President and Chief Executive Officer, Innopad, Inc.

"Insightful and easy to read - an indispensable Rosetta Stone for success in the high-technology capital equipment business."

- Bertrand Loy, Executive Vice President and Chief Operating Officer, Entegris, Inc.

"Unlike other product strategy and development books, *Equipped to Win* provides high-technology capital equipment managers with real life how-to steps and tools for managing products through their lifecycle. This handbook will be on tech leaders' desks, not their bookshelves!"

- Michael Luttati, Vice President of Global Services, Teradyne, Inc.

"Mike is one of the brightest marketing professionals I know. With *Equipped to Win*, he has given us an easy-to-read guide to the essentials and nuances of high-tech capital equipment product strategy, management, and marketing."

- Mitch Tyson, Chief Executive Officer, Advanced Electron Beams

"Mike Chase has written what our industry has needed for a long time - a straightforward guide that addresses the key issues facing high-tech capital equipment companies. It's a book you will appreciate immediately and revisit frequently."

- Greg Redinbo, Ph.D., Director of U.S. and Europe Sales, Varian Semiconductor Equipment Associates, Inc.

EQUIPPED TO WIN

Strategy, Product Management, and Marketing for High-Tech Capital Equipment Companies

By Michael Chase

Josh — Best of success to you! Michael Chase

Published by Tekcess International, LLC.

While it is the sincere intent of this publication to provide accurate and authoritative information in regard to the subject matter covered, the author and all those affiliated with the publication of this book assume no responsibility for events occurring to any person or entity taking action or refraining from taking action as a result of the material in this publication.

ISBN (Paperback): 978-0-557-27784-1

ISBN (Hardcover): 978-0-557-27785-8

CONTENTS

TABLES

Acknowledgements

Thank you to all of my colleagues, mentors, and clients. This book would not be possible if I weren't able to draw on the lessons that you have taught me and the experiences that we have shared.

My sincere appreciation goes to Ed Strenk, my editor, friend, and the best organizational development and sales training professional I've ever worked with. Many thanks for his dedication, ideas, and skill. It's impossible to overstate Ed's contribution to the readability and quality of this book. Many thanks also go to Cybele Grier, Ed's very capable assistant editor.

Above all, I want to thank my wife, Erin, for her patience, understanding, and support while I obsessed with writing this book.

Introduction

If you are a high-tech capital equipment executive frustrated with general-purpose strategy and marketing texts, this book is for you.

The concept for this book came to me a couple of years ago when I was working with a freshly minted product manager named Erik at a semiconductor equipment company. Erik, a bright Ph.D. who after over ten years on the technology development side of the house was making the transition into the world of marketing and product management.

After working together for just a couple of months, Erik came to me and said, "I find all of this extremely frustrating. I've read at least four different marketing and strategy books. They all describe what other companies have done, but none of them actually tell you how to do it for yourself. Furthermore, none of them seem to have anything to do with the type of business that we're in."

From the moment Erik spoke those words, I knew how I would approach writing this book.

You have in your hands the first ever how-to book that specifically addresses the unique challenges of the high-technology capital equipment industry.

Inside you will find clear, straightforward strategies, tactics, and tools to help you address your toughest strategy, product management, and marketing challenges. These are the same methods that I have used over a twenty-year, high-technology capital equipment career and continue to use at my consulting firm, Tekcess International.

This book puts the capital equipment industry's best practices at your fingertips. Whether it's how to get the most out of your aftermarket business, train the sales force, collect competitive intelligence, or keep product development programs on track, it's all here plus much more in a straightforward, how-to format.

I recommend that you scan this book cover to cover at least once to become familiar with its scope and the help it can provide. Then keep it somewhere within arm's reach at all times, ready to be referenced the next time a strategy, product management, or marketing problem crops up.

I hope you find that by reading this book and implementing the ideas it contains, you are better equipped than ever to succeed in the high-technology capital equipment business.

Enjoy

Part I: Strategy

1. How to Be More Strategic

As a high-technology capital equipment general manager or product line manager, it is easy to be completely consumed with the day-to-day tactics of running your business or product line. When this happens, it is nearly impossible for you to provide the strategic leadership required to ensure sustained growth and competitive advantage. If you are going to be successful over the long term, you need to figure out how to be more strategic.

The secret to resolving this is to set up a system that virtually automates the management of the day-to-day operation of your business or product line. Once you have the day-to-day issues under control, you need to understand how to use your free time to be more strategic. See figure 1.

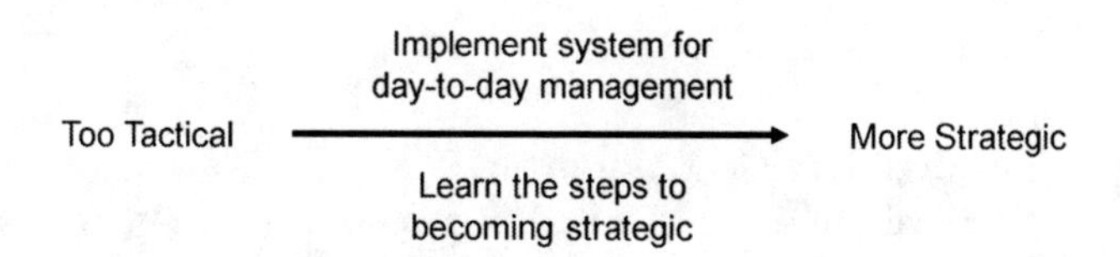

Figure 1: Process to Become More Strategic

Why It's Hard to Be Strategic

If you're like most general managers or product line managers of high-technology capital equipment companies, you spend most of your time chasing sales targets, solving customer issues, and tallying the quarter's numbers. You are probably spending precious little time developing competitive advantage, long-term growth strategy, or your organization.

Take a moment and think about it. How much time over the last month did you spend thinking about or working on strategic issues? If you find that you are consumed with the day-to-day, it's very possible that the processes and people capable of managing the tactical operations of your business haven't been fully developed. Until they are, you'll never be able to devote enough time to the things that will truly grow and improve your business.

The good news is that there are only five things you need to get under control. Once you do, you'll be able to spend more time solving the truly strategic issues facing your company.

First, Get the Day-to-Day Under Control

A high-technology business has only five core processes. Develop and implement the infrastructure to manage them, and you are on your way to spending more time working on growing your business. The five things are:

1. Financial Reporting
2. Sales
3. Revenue
4. Product Development
5. Customer Service

Financial reporting encompasses all of the management and external financial reporting required to run your business. Sales is made up of orders and the outlook for orders. The revenue process includes everything the organization does to turn an order into revenue such as manufacturing, testing, and shipping. Product development refers to the management and tracking of current development programs. And finally, customer service refers to all of the activity associated with making sure that customers are happy with your products once they receive them.

Effective businesses need to know the current status of each process at all times. For example, you always need to know where you stand against quarterly profit, sales, and revenue goals. Without a process in place that routinely produces this information, 100 percent of your time can be consumed with constantly trying to assemble the latest status.

The way out is to delegate the daily management of these processes to a competent, functional team and to establish a routine that consistently produces accurate and timely information. You must hire and develop a functional staff that you can truly rely on to manage the performance for each of the five processes. If you lack confidence in your team, you will find yourself drawn back into the tactical management of the daily operations. There is absolutely no substitute for hiring a functional staff that is 100 percent competent and comfortable managing these processes. Do not compromise here.

The next step is to build a business dashboard that will provide all of the key indicators for each of the five processes. Similar to the way a car's dashboard indicates the health of the car, your dashboard should indicate the health of your business. Your business or product line dashboard will vary depending on the nature of your specific operation, but it will typically contain elements like those in table 1.

Once you've established the elements required in each of the dashboards, have each functional owner create a concise report—often just one page—that will communicate the current status of the processes in their respective dashboards.

Often, the best approach is to utilize your weekly staff meeting to review performance on each of the five business processes. Your agenda literally becomes the five things with each owner presenting his or her dashboard.

Table 1: Business Process Dashboard Elements

Business Process	**Example Contents**
Financial Reporting	• Quarterly P&L versus Goal • Quarterly P&L versus Current Quarter Forecast
Sales	• Quarterly Bookings versus Goals • Quarterly Bookings versus Current Quarter Forecast
Revenue	• Quarterly Revenue versus Goal • Quarterly Revenue versus Current Quarter Forecast
Product Development	• Status versus Milestones • Status versus Success Criteria
Customer Service	• Installations Status • Customer Down Status and Action Plan

Hold your meeting on a regular schedule, and keep to the agenda without deep dives on technical issues, budget reviews, or customer issue resolution. Set up specific meetings to deal with anything outside of the five things. Your objective is to institutionalize a habit, set expectations, and establish accountability. Nothing does that better than being consistent and persistent. If you can't make your staff meeting for a legitimate reason, delegate the meeting to a staff member and insist on receiving the updated reports after the meeting. You must maintain the routine in order to create the organizational habit.

Keep refining the process until your organization has matured and can routinely and effortlessly produce accurate status on your dashboard. Issues will still be escalated to you, but these will be the exception, not the rule.

Imagine walking out of your staff meeting every week with the answers to everything that your CEO is likely to ask, and with the confidence that your team is managing the daily operations of your business. You should feel an immediate sense of control, and a sense of freedom to spend time on your strategic issues.

From Fire Fighter to Strategic Leader

You're now free to spend your time cultivating growth opportunities, resolving the truly critical issues, improving your competitive position, and developing your organization. But how do you get started?

To be strategic, you're still going to turn to the five processes, but look at them through the strategy lens, not the tactical lens. That lens is characterized by an external perspective and a time horizon greater than day-to-day. When you accomplish this, the questions that you worry about will change, as shown in table 2.

Since you've established the team and process that manages everything in the tactical column, you can now spend time thinking about the strategic issues affecting each part of your business. Of course, thinking about them isn't enough; you'll want to figure out what the most critical strategic issues are and act on them.

It's easy to be at a loss for how to get started. Strategic issues by their nature are not urgent, so there's no immediate pressure to resolve them. Shifting gears to a strategic mindset is actually pretty difficult, especially if you've grown accustomed to fighting the fire of the day and getting the instant gratification that comes with putting it out.

A product manager once said to me, "I'm so busy supporting day-to-day sales issues that I don't have time to be strategic."

I asked him, "If all of your sales support tasks were eliminated right this minute, so that you could immediately focus 100 percent on strategy, what's the first thing you'd do?"

Table 2: Tactical vs. Strategic Questions

Business Process	**Instead of Tactical Questions …**	**Try Strategic Questions …**
Financial Reporting	Are we going to make the quarter?	What's causing the margin erosion over the last three years in Asia?
Sales	What price is required to close this order?	Why are some customers willing to pay more for our system than others?
Revenue	Where is the last part we need in order to make the shipment on time?	Why are our competitor's inventory turns twice ours?
Product Development	Is the product demonstration ready to run this Friday?	What do we need to address for our customers' next generation devices?
Customer Service	How will we get that system in China back up and running?	How can we use service to create competitive barriers to entry?

"I don't know," he said.

The concept of strategic thinking can be so abstract that we're often not sure where to begin. What you need is a framework to guide you, so that you don't go back to your desk and just stare at your computer screen when the fire fighting stops. The straightforward, six-step process in table 3 will help you sort through your strategic issues and develop specific action plans to address them.

Table 3: Steps to Taking Action on Strategic Issues

Step	Action
1	Identify the strategic issues for each of the five business processes; write each down in the form of a question. For example, "How can we use service to create competitive barriers to entry?"
2	When finished, select which strategic issue(s) you need to tackle.
3	Determine what information is needed to understand the issue and figure out where you can get the information.
4	Gather the information and analyze it.
5	Create an objective statement for what must be done. For example, "Automate consumable parts replenishment and ordering for our five largest customers."
6	Develop an achievable action plan.

You're probably not going to breeze through the six steps on your own. What will happen, though, is that you'll start engaging the organization on matters of strategic importance instead of just the daily fire fighting. Whether it's identifying strategic issues, agreeing on the most important ones, or putting a team together to tackle one, you'll have made the transition from fire fighter to strategic leader.

2. Five Strategy Errors and How to Avoid Them

Defining and implementing a strategy is hard work. In the day-to-day battle with demanding customers and aggressive competitors, most of us don't get a chance to really perfect the strategic planning process. This chapter will get you off on the right foot by helping you recognize and avoid five of the most common strategy development and implementation errors that companies make. Those five errors are:

1. Confusing strategy with tactics
2. Working inside-out instead of outside-in
3. Operating with vague vision
4. Failing to identify the "won't do's"
5. Not instituting strategy management controls

Let's take a look at each of these in detail.

Confusing Strategy with Tactics

Every business has pressing issues, but which ones are actually strategic? Are falling sales a strategic issue? What about rising material costs? Or a new competitor?

Knowing how to distinguish between strategic and tactical issues is critical to any strategy development effort. Otherwise, your effort could be overrun by tactics and you may never produce anything that is actually strategic.

Perceptions of exactly what constitutes strategy can be very diverse even among a single management team. A single question about strategy can produce multiple perspectives that must be resolved before attempting to make any meaningful strategy decisions. The following story and dialogue with a Tekcess International client helps illustrate this point.

"In this year's strategic plan, I want to re-examine our sales compensation structure and understand why we spend so much on system demonstrations, and I want a new deal approval process in place."

That's the answer I got from a capital equipment company senior manager in response to the question, "What are the most important things to address in this year's strategic plan?"

Continuing my senior management interviews, I met with the Senior VP of Marketing and asked the same question.

His response: "That's easy. In two years, our customers will be manufacturing their next-generation device. This will make our current system obsolete. We will have a hole in our portfolio if we don't do something."

The marketing executive had a very different perspective on the year's strategic plan. The first executive looked internally to find the most important issues. On the other hand, the Marketing VP looked externally for emerging threats to the business.

A third executive answered the question this way.

"We're not going to do anything strategic this year. We need to work on our current business before we think about another acquisition."

With this third executive came yet a third perspective. In his view, an issue wasn't strategic unless it involved an acquisition, implying that any issues in the existing business must be tactical.

Why the three completely different perspectives on the same question? It's simple; the management team was asked to identify strategic issues before they had a common definition of the word "strategy."

An effective strategy definition should clearly distinguish between strategy and tactics. To that end, consider the following:

Strategy is the big decisions that senior managers make to respond to or anticipate changes in the market or the competitive environment. Everything else is tactics.

Notice that this definition lays out a much clearer concept of strategy than the typical "strategy is long term, and tactics are short term" paradigm. It sets strategy apart from tactics on two key dimensions:

1. Decisions vs. actions
2. External vs. internal perspective

A definition like this fosters a strategic mindset, and when used as a filter, it will help keep tactical issues from distracting your strategy development efforts.

If you're going to embark on a strategy development exercise, step one is to get everyone on the same page as to what the strategic issues are. First, ask your strategy team to write down all of the issues that need to be addressed during strategy development. Have them write each issue on a separate yellow sticky-note. Don't put any constraints on this step; let everyone get their issues on the table unfiltered. When they have finished, have them post all of the issues on one wall.

Then, present the strategy definition to the team.

Next, put the word "Tactics" on a large piece of flipchart paper and post it on another wall. Have everyone re-examine the original issues against your common definition of strategy.

Those issues that don't pass the "strategic" test get moved to the tactics wall. What remains are the strategic issues that need to be addressed during strategy development.

Remember to save the tactical issues. They still need to be addressed once the strategy is defined, and you start detailed action planning.

Working Inside-out Instead of Outside-in

Developing an effective strategy follows a deliberate sequence of phases. These phases start from the outside perspective and work their way inward to specific decisions that you must make. Strategy is all about deciding what to do about changes in your market and how your competitors are responding. If you get this process backward and work from the inside out, your strategy will end up describing what you can do rather than what you need to do. There's nothing wrong with knowing your capabilities and strengths, but it's critical to know what you need to do in order to beat the competition and meet market needs first.

In its simplest form, strategy development follows three phases, and in each, you're trying to answer just three fundamental questions. See table 4.

The answers to the first two questions frame the external or outside perspective that you need in order to develop an effective strategy. In the environment phase, you're looking for changes in market requirements and the potential technologies available to address them. In the situation phase, you're comparing your company's capability versus those market requirements and your competitors' ability to address them.

Table 4: Strategy Development Phases and Key Questions

Phase	Description	Question
1.	Environment	What are our opportunities and strategic issues?
2.	Situation	Where do we stand vs. those opportunities and issues?
3.	Strategy	What decisions must we make?

After these two questions are answered, you're ready to start developing your strategy. Figure 2 depicts the top-level, capital equipment strategic planning process used by Tekcess International. Notice that the steps associated with strategy development don't begin until after the external analysis in phases one and two is complete.

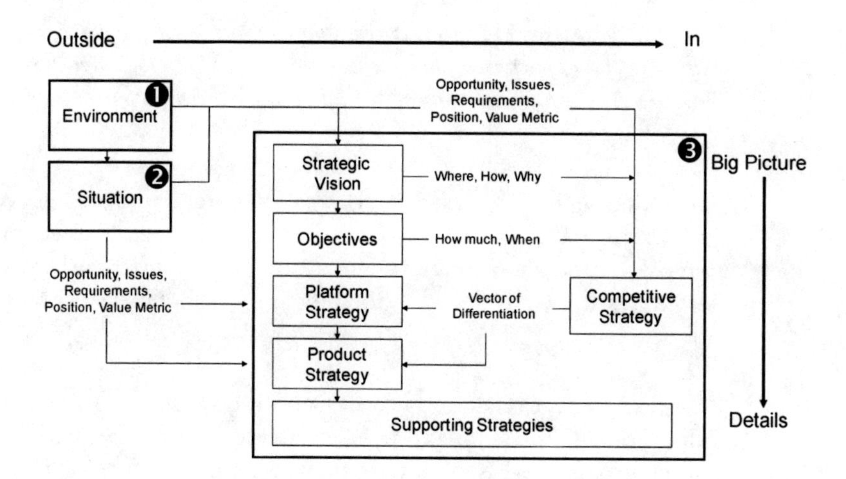

Figure 2: Strategy Development Process

When it comes to the strategy phase itself, the order of the strategy development steps is critical to ensure that the strategy is aligned to address your markets and attack your competitors.

Strategy is developed with increasing levels of specificity at each step, from strategic vision all the way down to detailed supporting strategies. This funnel approach serves two purposes. It forces big picture thinking before the conversations get cluttered with lower level details. It also forces detailed product and supporting strategies to fit a strategic framework.

If you execute these phases and steps in any other order or attempt to complete them in parallel, you'll find yourself trying to do just the opposite. You'll be trying to fit a strategic framework to your details, plans, and tactics. This will derail the process and keep your team from uncovering and attacking the true strategic issues that will determine your company's success.

Operating with Vague Vision

Many companies lose their way on the road to success because their strategic vision is so vague that it fails to provide a framework for strategy. Take for example the vision statement below, which is supposed to describe a company's future.

We will become a leading equipment supplier to the semiconductor industry by listening to our customers and meeting their needs. At the same time, we will maximize return to our shareholders and provide a rewarding work environment for our employees.

It sounds good, it reads well, and its core messages are easy to remember. But it lacks specific information and direction that employees need in order to move the company toward its desired state. It's full of feel-good thoughts, but distinctly silent on strategic direction.

A good strategic vision, however, is both destination and direction. It aligns the organization and focuses efforts to drive the success of the company. It also sets the framework for platform and product strategy. A good strategic vision outlines:

- Where you are going
- What path you will take

- Why you will win[i]

Take for example this vision statement:

We will:

- *Be the number one supplier of thin film deposition systems to the semiconductor market.*
- *Leverage our core competency in deposition source technologies across multiple semiconductor equipment platforms.*
- *Produce the fastest deposition rates and as a result, the lowest cost of ownership for our customers.*

Table 5 shows how this statement can be decomposed into the key components of good strategic vision.

Table 5: Vision Statement by Component

Component	**Vision**
Where you are going	We will be the number one supplier of thin film deposition systems to the semiconductor market.
What path you will take	We will leverage our core competency in deposition source technologies across multiple semiconductor equipment platforms.
Why you will win	We will produce the fastest deposition rates and as a result, the lowest cost of ownership for our customers.

Compared to the vague vision, this vision is clear and precise. It directs employees' actions and behaviors in very specific ways that will drive total organizational alignment. This vision statement also successfully establishes the framework for platform and product strategy. Just from the vision statement, you know that you'll be investing in deposition source technology to create multiple products to beat the competition with the fastest deposition rates and the lowest cost of ownership.

Notice also that this vision statement is written at a business-unit or market-segment level. Targeting vision statements at this level works best. Attempting to define a vision statement at the corporate level for a multi-segment company often results in a statement that's so watered down that it loses its ability to provide direction to the organization.

Failing to Identify the "Won't Do's"

It's common to see everyone's heads bobbing up and down with approving smiles as grand strategies are being formulated to beat the competition. However, smiles quickly turn to frowns when you start explicitly outlining the "won't do's" so that you can keep the organization focused on the strategy. Here's where the real tough decision making rears its head.

Doing everything is the antithesis of strategy. Strategy is as much about deciding what not to do as it is deciding what to do. Strategies don't really take on real meaning until the management team has reached consensus on what they will not do. It's those "won't do's" that really test the discipline of an organization. Failing to do this almost assures that some portion of your organization will be distracted from your core mission. Your strategy needs to identify:

- Markets or customers that you won't chase.
- Product features that you won't implement.
- Products that you won't continue to produce.

The test of an organization's strategic discipline is how they behave in the last week of the quarter when one of your "won't do" customers pops up to buy your "won't do" end-of-life product, requesting just a few small "won't do" product features.

Not Instituting Strategy Management Controls

When you ask managers the reason why they view strategic planning as a waste of time, one of the most common responses is, "Once the planning process is complete, it gets put on a shelf or sent to the board of directors, and then we go about fighting our daily fires as usual."

This is a common problem that most companies try to address with formal communication programs plus linked rewards and compensation plans. There's nothing wrong with this approach; however, it's usually not enough to keep the strategy on track. What's needed is strategy management and control integration with the management and control mechanisms that already exist in your company.

You probably already have a regular heartbeat of operations and product development reviews to make sure that you're meeting near-term targets. To avoid adding unnecessary overhead, try integrating strategy monitoring into an existing business or product line review instead of creating another meeting for strategy management. To integrate strategy control into an existing review, just add these elements to keep your strategy on track:

- Current multi-year market forecast
- Changes in market environment
- Outlook for market share
- Status on key accounts/markets needed to hit share goals
- Changes in competitive environment
- Product performance roadmap vs. competition
- Current development status on each product roadmap item

Adding a review of key strategy elements to your existing management and control systems not only creates the inspection point to make sure that things stay on track, but it also keeps the strategy and situation data current. As a result, you'll have a much more robust starting point when you hit the next planning cycle.

3. The Three Phases of Capital Equipment Industry Maturity

Are you the only game in town? Are you the only company that can meet your customers' most advanced requirements? If you are, consider yourself lucky, but don't get too comfortable.

High-technology capital equipment industries mature through three very predictable phases. These three phases can be described as:

1. Can you do it?
2. How fast can you do it?
3. Everything else.

Each phase has a different competitive environment, requires a different strategic approach, and produces a different profit profile. Business also gets tougher as markets mature, but there are ways to prepare your company to handle the challenges and opportunities in each phase.

So, let's take a look at how these three industry phases will drive changes in your strategy.

Phase 1: Can You Do It?

This occurs when you're the only supplier who can meet the market's technical requirements, the only player "who can do it." Living in this phase is usually the result of a technological breakthrough or market inflection, which redefines a market or enables a new one.

Profits are bountiful in this phase, because if you are the only solution, pricing tends toward the threshold of value brought to the market as opposed to an extremely competitive environment, where pricing tends toward minimal, acceptable margins.

The best companies recognize this and aim their competitive strategy to ensure that they thrive in this phase as long as possible. They do this by knowing their customers and their problems better than the competition. They develop solutions to those problems before their competitors even know that the problem exists. Then, they build intellectual property (IP) barriers around their solution to protect their position. The companies most successful at lingering in the "Can You Do It?" phase usually exhibit the following characteristics:

- Invest heavily in application and process engineering.
- Engage systematically with customers' technology development groups.
- Focus on IP strategy, both offensive and defensive.

The problem is that as your competitors are watching you rake in the profits, they become obsessed with getting a piece of the action. Because the profit potential is so tempting to competitors, your lifespan in this phase can be brief unless you are constantly investing to renew your position.

Phase 2: How Fast Can You Do It?

Eventually, one of your hungry competitors will figure out a way around your IP and develop an alternative solution. The second they do it, you've entered stage two of market maturity.

With more than one player able to meet key technical requirements, capital equipment suppliers will have to compete primarily on cost of ownership metrics, which are usually dominated by some measure of productivity or throughput. Productivity is defined as equipment output of your customer's product per unit of time. This is why Phase 2 gets the name, "How fast can you do it?"

Margins are still fairly decent if you can maintain a productivity advantage, since each increment in improved cost of ownership or throughput can be translated directly into value for the customer. In fact, pricing in this phase has a direct correlation to productivity. The least productive suppliers will typically achieve the minimally acceptable margin to keep their businesses operating. This sets the floor for pricing. More productive offerings will achieve a pricing premium over this level directly proportional to their productivity advantage. This relationship is shown in figure 3.

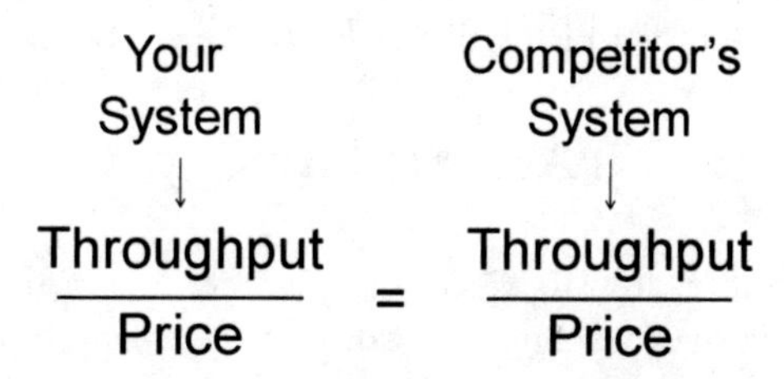

Figure 3: Price and Throughput Relationship

This phase lasts until the throughput saturates, meaning the customer no longer benefits from further throughput improvements. For example, if you're an equipment manufacturer and your throughput is so high that a single machine in your customer's factory is sufficient, the customer won't value further throughput improvements. At this point, Phase 3 takes hold.

Phase 3: Everything Else.

Business starts to get tougher here. Now you are largely competing on the ownership experience. Pricing pressure is intense. Spare parts availability, ease of transaction, reliability, applications support, and customer service responsiveness all become critical. Margins shrink dramatically.

Typically, in this phase end markets are maturing and technological changes are slowing. You can tell if you're in the "Everything Else" phase by the following:

- Discussions around the office are more about operational efficiency than innovation.
- There is increased emphasis on aftermarket revenue.
- Your company has announced its first ever stock dividend.

This is the plateau of a high-technology industry or segment. The final phase of consolidation happens here, and the market share of the remaining participants is likely to stabilize. The last remaining players may make a decent living, but they will find themselves eliminated from growth fund managers' "Stocks-to-Watch" lists.

Know Where You Are; Set Strategy Accordingly

It's important to recognize where you are and to align your competitive strategies to address the challenges of each market phase.

If you are in the "Can You Do It?" phase, do everything you can to protect your position and prolong it. Brainstorm how a competitor may enter the space or circumvent your IP. Then, build a defensive IP barricade around those possibilities, even if you have no intention of implementing them. Also, invest to extend your current position and to keep your competitors perpetually a lap or two behind.

If you've moved on to the "How Fast Can You Do It?" phase, recognize that this is a cost of ownership play, and make sure that product strategies push for at least a 25 percent advantage over your competition. As a rule of thumb, this is the threshold needed to affect market share shifts and achieve a price premium. This is important because you are going to need commanding market share as you enter the final phase to ensure that you're the last company standing.

When you finally hit the "Everything Else" phase, you should be well down the path developing growth options outside your core business. You'll need a new growth engine to propel your company as your core business levels off. You need to defend your core business aggressively, but you also need to start diverting profits to fund the next big thing.

The strategies to drive your business in each the three phases is summarized in Table 6.

Table 6: Strategy by Industry Phase

Phase	Compete on	Strategy
Can you do it?	Unique capability	Develop defensive IP and other barriers to entry.
How fast can you do it?	Cost of ownership	Invest to maintain >25% productivity advantage.
Everything else.	Reliability, service levels, price	Shift R&D (Research and Development) spending to new growth options.

4. Strategic Issues and Disruptions

You've been there. The VP of Marketing is at the front of the room with the projector beam coloring her face different shades of blue, yellow, and red as she scrolls through chart after chart with northeast trending forecasts.

"Here we go again," you think to yourself. "We've seen this before, but we have real issues, and if we don't tackle them, all this talk of opportunity is senseless."

Too often, the strategic planning process focuses on the opportunities and possibilities for greatness with limited attention focused on addressing the true strategic issues and potential disruptions that can bring a company to its knees. When this happens, you run the risk that the whole strategic planning effort will end up a paper exercise, with little or no impact on the business.

To fully engage your team in the strategic planning process and make a fundamental difference to your business performance, you have to begin with identifying the issues and disruptions that your business needs to address.

What are Strategic Issues?

Strategic issues are those things that will prevent the organization from reaching its long-term goals. They are not the day-to-day fire fights like customer satisfaction hiccups or product problems. Strategic issues are caused by changes in the market or competitive environment that, over time, will impair the organization's ability to be successful. Examples of strategic issues might be:

- 90 percent of your business is in Asia where local competitors are emerging with lower cost structures, better cultural alignment, and better access to your customers.
- Your market growth rate has slowed to less than 8 percent, and if you don't find a way to renew growth, your stock value will decline as your company stock's price-to-earnings ratio contracts.
- Since your major competitor has entered the market, prices have significantly eroded; if this keeps up, you won't be able to sustain the research and development necessary to remain competitive.
- Your largest, fastest-growing market is China, but the government limits export of your products; your foreign competitors don't face this dilemma.

Notice that each example deals with a long-term macro, externally caused predicament. Unless you deal with these issues in the strategic planning process, they will get lost in the daily fire fighting.

Disruptions? What Disruptions?

Disruptions are those seismic shifts that fundamentally shake the relevance of your business. Most often, these disruptions are a result of technology changes. These usually come in two varieties:

- Disruptions to your end market that affect its size or existence
- Disruptions in the technologies that satisfy your market

The world of high technology is by nature full of disruptions. They must be anticipated and addressed in the strategic planning process, or you'll wake up one day and find your business facing obsolescence. Consider these examples:

- CD's displace cassette tapes.
- MP3's trump CD's.
- Fiber optic rolls over copper.
- VOIP obsoletes Ma Bell.
- Flash memory erases hard drives.
- Copper pushes aluminum out of CMOS.
- Compact Florescent Lights (CFL's) challenge incandescents.
- High Brightness LED's take on CFL's.

To get a jump start on your list of potential disruptions to your business:

- Review proceedings from recent technical conferences relevant to your marketplace.
- Make sure you know what your industry's leaders and most promising start-up companies are working on.

You need to pay attention to those new technologies that have a high probability of broad adoption and if adopted, would have significant impact on your business.

Defining Critical Issues and Disruptions

Most strategic planning processes start with an environmental analysis phase followed by a situation or competitive analysis. It's in these phases that the critical issues and disruptions are catalogued. Force each of these phases to conclude with a list of critical issues and disruptions that must be addressed in the strategic plan. Sample outlines for the first two planning phases are shown in figure 4.

Notice that both the environmental and situation analysis end with a summary of the most critical issues. This focuses the organization on those elements of the environment and your situation that must be addressed in your strategy. For each of these, it is necessary to spell out the implications to your company and the time frame in which it needs to be addressed. A sample template for this process is shown in figure 5.

Environmental Analysis Outline

- Customer's Environment
  - Market growth drivers
  - Market size, segments, and growth
  - Technology trends and disruptions
- Our Environment
  - Market growth drivers
  - Market size, segments, and growth
  - Market's top spenders
  - Technology trends and disruptions
- Summary
  - Most critical issues

Situation Analysis Outline

- Market Position
  - Historical financials
  - Historical market share
  - Position in top spenders
- Market Requirements
  - Position vs. market requirements
- Competition
  - Summary of competitors
  - Competitive position
  - IP position
- Summary
  - Most critical issues

Figure 4: Environmental and Situation Analysis Outline

Critical Issue or Disruption	Implications for <Company>	Timing		
		≤2011	2012 2013	>2013
1.				
2.				
3.				
4.				
N.				

Figure 5: Template for Recording Critical Issues and Implications

It is often effective to assign ownership for this process to the CTO or lead technologist in your organization along with the lead marketing executive. A thorough examination of each potential issue and disruption is required to determine the probability, likely timing, and potential repercussions for your business. Those that are likely to have an impact on your business make the final cut, and you need to assign key business leaders as owners for each.

In this initial phase of your planning, you won't try to address the specific issues and disruptions. That will come later in the process when you begin to define your strategy. Your objective at this phase is just to get your team's consensus on the definition of the key issues and a commitment to address them in the strategic plan.

Strategic Plan with Real Impact

By identifying and addressing the true strategic issues and potential disruptions to your business, you'll have a head start on a strategic plan that will drive your business in the right direction. These issues, combined with your strategic objectives and platform strategy, provide a framework for your product strategy.

Taking the time to identify the most critical strategic business issues will also align and energize your team because they'll know that they will be solving real problems that will show measurable results. As a result, you will be on your way to winning over your most cynical strategic-planning critics.

5. Less is More

Most companies have a vision that begins with a phrase like; "To be the leading supplier of product X to the Y market…."

Some realize their vision; some don't.

Those that do, usually have a very clearly defined target market. They understand its needs better than anyone and focus all of their efforts on satisfying them.

Those that don't, often have such a vague definition of their market that almost any prospect fits it. As a result, they end up burdened with a punch-list of disparate customer needs. In contrast, those that achieve market leadership understand the "Less is more" concept better than most.

Don't Chase Every Prospect

Guided by sales goals or fears of missing an opportunity, there's a temptation to try to capture any piece of business that enters the sales pipeline.

Imagine this scenario.

You're a process equipment manufacturer for the semiconductor industry. It's a cyclical industry and you happen to currently be in a deep downturn. Your target markets, mainstream memory and logic manufacturers, are just not buying.

Along comes a manufacturer of automotive devices. To make their devices, they use process equipment like yours, but they use a non-standard wafer type that will require you to design a special wafer handling option. Over the last fifteen years, this prospect has only purchased two systems like yours. But now, they have money and need a third.

Business is so slow that taking the order is very tempting because the order will generate short-term revenue and might even save the quarter.

Before taking the order, you need to think about the potential cost to your company by considering:

- Design and test costs for the special wafer option
- On-going field inventory carrying costs for the special spare parts
- Depreciation cost of an engineering test stand and support tooling
- Additional test development, documentation, and training costs
- On-going support for a special software configuration
- "End of life" management for the unique parts
- Opportunity costs of not focusing on your core business

I think you can see how every time you stray from your target market to capture short-term revenue, you create new long-term product performance and support obligations. Each one of these dilutes your ability to achieve your core vision. The more customers you're chasing and supporting that don't fit in your target market, the less likely you are to achieve a leadership position in any market.

Target and Non-Target Markets

Of course, you can't tell if a customer is in or out of your target market if you haven't clearly defined it. What you're looking for is a market segment big enough to support your financial objectives with lots of customers who have similar buying behaviors and product needs. Once you've found it, define it as precisely as possible.

Next, with the same precision, you need to define which segments you will not chase, because they are not as valuable, won't value your offering, or are better served by your competitors.

However, clearly defining target and non-target markets is only half the battle.

Let's use the previous example to prove the point. Let's assume this automotive device maker was not in your target market. You knew it, but really hadn't invested in making sure that the rest of the organization did. You have set the stage for the following to happen.

The sales manager will find this opportunity and contact inside sales to get a quote. They, in turn, will ask engineering to develop a design concept and cost estimate. While this is progressing and eating up resources and time, the sales manager will go back to the customer to let him know that the factory is working on a proposal. This flurry of activity will culminate with inside sales dropping the proposal on your desk for your signature.

You, of course, won't sign off because this customer, with his special request to handle a non-standard wafer, is outside your target market.

Two very bad things happen. First, a good-sized effort was put into chasing an order that the company never intended to accept. Second, the sales manager must now go back to the customer and explain that there has been a change in plans. The result of not having everyone on the same page is wasted effort and a stain on the company's credibility and reputation.

The second half of the battle is to get organizational consensus on both target and non-target markets. Once that's achieved, stop all work and prospecting in non-target markets, then align your whole organization to understand and serve your target market better than anybody else. It seems counter intuitive, but by doing less, you will actually achieve more.

It's a Matter of Leverage

The concept of leverage is to produce a large result from a small effort. This is also the essence of the "Less is more" concept. When a company chases a lot of small results, like the automotive device manufacturer in our example, the effort is not leveraged. Companies that are distracted by low leverage pursuits will fall behind their more focused competitors.

Let me try to illustrate again using our example.

The top five customers in your target market typically buy one hundred machines a year combined. They now have an emerging requirement for temperature-controlled processing. This new capability will be required by the whole market over the next two years, but customers are evaluating suppliers right now during the downturn. This new capability requires about the same effort as developing the non-standard wafer option for the automotive device manufacturer.

You and your competitor have typically split your target market right down the middle. The supplier that is first to market with a temperature-controlled processing solution stands to disrupt this historical 50-50 split. The stakes are high. Each of the top five customers is worth twenty system sales a year.

I think you're starting to get the picture. Meeting the automotive manufacturer's non-standard wafer requirement in our example will at most produce a system sale every five years. This is very low leverage. Beating your competition in the race to meet the new temperature-controlled process requirement in your target market produces twenty machines a year for every customer captured. This is very high leverage.

"Wait a minute," you say. "Why not do both?" You could. But who is likely to win the race to satisfy the new requirement in your target market? The company with laser beam focus, or the one chasing every opportunity? What if you lose?

Less Is More Case Study

When I started working with this particular capital equipment company, they were losing a lot of money, shedding market share, and trying to fix their abysmal product quality.

Not wanting to let any opportunity slip by, they were chasing six different market applications for their thin film deposition system. While each of these applications used their basic type of equipment, each had very different performance and configuration requirements. There were almost as many engineering projects as there were engineers.

After conducting a quick analysis, it became clear that one of the six markets was two times larger than the remaining five combined. And as luck would have it, the company's thin film system had fundamental competitive advantages in that one large market.

The direction that we needed to take seemed pretty clear. After achieving consensus with the leadership team, we:

- Stopped all work and put together a plan to unwind existing commitments in the five smaller market segments.
- Shifted all sales, marketing, and engineering efforts to the one large segment.

I can still remember being barraged with aggressive questions at the all-employee meeting where I unveiled the strategy. To the organization, it seemed heresy to narrow our prospects when we were in such bad shape. I fielded, "What about..." and, "Yeah, but…" questions for almost an hour before everyone got the idea that I was serious.

By everyone sticking to the plan and working on our best opportunity, we achieved the following results in short order.

- Reduced total expenses, but increased funding for target market projects.
- Fostered much better relationships with our customers than the competition had.
- Matured the product from a dog to a top performer.

One year after that all-employee meeting, the business turned profitable, market position was a strong number two, and instead of being a drag on the corporation, this business unit was one of its best prospects for growth.

Less really is more.

6. The Power of the Value Metric

A sales vice president for a high-technology, capital equipment company summed up the problem when he said to me, "Our marketing team talks eloquently about our product's technical features. But, they don't give me anything that shows how our customers will make more money buying our system over the competitor's. That's what I really need in order to win and justify pricing."

Value Is a Financial Expression

To find out if you have the same problem at your company, try this with your marketing team. Ask them, "What is our value proposition?"

You might get something like, "Our unique technology provides 30 percent better uniformity than the competition does."

This is a bad answer. Your unique technology is a means to create value, but it does not represent value by itself. Any answer that does not include some expression of currency is off the mark. That's because value is a financial expression. The only reason why your customers buy your equipment is to make money. When they're deciding between two suppliers, they're going to buy from the one that they believe will make them the most. It only follows that you need to be driving product strategy to develop an advantage in financial value for your customer, and of course marketing strategies and tools to articulate it.

After providing this short lesson to that same marketing team, you should re-ask the question and hopefully this time get an answer like this:

"Our unique technology provides 30 percent better uniformity than the competition, resulting in ten more salable units per day. At $1,000 profit per unit and 330 production days per year, our machine produces $3.3 million more profit each year for our customers."

In the first answer, no financial value was expressed; in the second, it's clear that your product is worth $3.3 million more a year than the competitor's product is worth.

Defining Your Value Metric

Your job as the supplier is to understand exactly how your customer profits from your product. Then this needs to be quantified and expressed as your "Value Metric."

In its most generic form, your Value Metric is the revenue that your customer can earn with your product, divided by your product's price and operating costs. The exact parameters in this equation depend on the nature of your specific product or service, but in general a Value Metric is expressed as in figure 6:

$$\frac{\text{Price/unit} \times \text{Yield} \times \text{Throughput} \times \text{Uptime}}{\text{System Price} + \text{Operating Costs}}$$

Figure 6: General Value Metric Expression

The terms in the Value Metric expression are as follows:

- Price/unit is the price that the customer can achieve from each unit of their product.
- Yield is the percentage of good units that your system produces out of the total processed.
- Throughput is the rate at which your system produces product.
- Uptime is the percentage of time that your system is available for production and not in a repair or maintenance state.
- System price is the selling price of your system.
- Operating costs are all of the costs associated with running your system, such as utilities and source materials.

Buyers of capital equipment need to do an exhaustive cost of ownership calculation in order to create capital and expense budgets and profit forecasts. They need to arrive at an exact operating cost and, as a result, need to capture and understand every element that constitutes the cost of ownership. The capital equipment supplier does not.

When defining the Value Metric for your product, focus on your customer's primary selection criteria and the competitive issues for your industry. Let's say you're a supplier of ion implanters, a piece of semiconductor process equipment used for transistor formation. The first step in creating your Value Metric is to determine which elements of the general expression are part of your customer's primary selection criteria for an ion implanter. Table 7 shows one possible scenario of "what is" and "what is not" critical to the decision to buy an ion implanter.

In this example, buyers primarily select ion implanters on throughput, uptime, and system price. A "no" next to price/unit, yield, and operating costs says that for all suppliers these are about the same, and they do not have a major impact on the buying decision. In this example, your Value Metric might be as simple as is shown in figure 7.

You don't need to fully analyze every detailed element that contributes to the value expression. Remember, this is an exercise for understanding value as your customer sees it when comparing you to your competitors; it is not a comprehensive cost of ownership modeling exercise.

Table 7: Value Metric Element vs. Primary Selection Criteria Example

Value Metric Element	Primary Selection Criteria?	Value Metric Element	Primary Selection Criteria?
Price/Unit	No	Uptime	Yes
Throughput	Yes	System Price	Yes
Yield	No	Operating Costs	No

$$\frac{\text{Throughput x Uptime}}{\text{System Price}}$$

Figure 7: Example Value Metric with Only Primary Selection Criteria

Shape Product Strategy Using the Value Metric

Before value can be sold, it must be created. Sounds obvious, but for some reason the world is filled with "how to sell value" books and seminars, but little is ever written about how to create it.

Value is created by maximizing your value expressed by your Value Metric. To do this, you need to understand how each performance specification of your product contributes to each element of the value expression. Then, set new product roadmap performance targets so that they will meet customer requirements at introduction and result in a Value Metric substantially higher than that of your competitor.

This concept is very helpful when working through the trade-offs between performance specifications, technology risks, costs, and development time for a new product. The value expression approach typically describes a broad solution space that can be satisfied with many performance specification combinations.

For example, maybe the throughput target specified by marketing is difficult or costly to achieve, but exceeding the yield target or lowering operating costs is easy. Run the numbers. If the target value can still be created, you may have found another solution.

By focusing on value creation instead of achieving a particular specification, you'll uncover more options for creating competitive advantage.

Set Performance Targets Using the Value Metric

Ever spend millions of dollars and tens of months developing a new product, only to find yourself in the same competitive position as when you started? Maybe the market yawned at the improvements you made, the competition made more progress than you anticipated, or perhaps the program came up a little short.

It doesn't have to be that way. You can develop products that really move the needle. The secret lies in understanding how to set new product performance targets and manage the inevitable trade-offs that crop up during development.

One of the first things to understand when setting product performance targets is how to apply the 25 percent rule. This rule states the following.

Market share and/or pricing don't improve appreciably unless you have at least a 25 percent value advantage over your competition.

Two things are at work here. First of all, new customers need a real incentive to take on the risks and costs of switching suppliers. If your value is in the general vicinity of an incumbent competitor, you're not going to get the customer's attention. Unless the customer can see the potential for a step-function improvement, it's safer and cheaper for her to just stay with the competition.

Second, customers will discount your claims. You say 25 percent advantage; customers think maybe 15 percent. As your claimed advantage starts to drop below 25 percent, you find yourself quickly "in the noise." When your equipment is labeled "not much different," you won't be rewarded with higher pricing or a decision to dump the competition.

Like you, your competition isn't standing still. They, too, have a roadmap and are spending R&D dollars to make it happen. A 25 percent advantage over their performance today is not 25 percent a year from now. So how do you decide where to set performance targets?

First you'll need to assemble an estimate of your competitors' roadmap as best you can. The most important competitor to analyze is the industry benchmark, or highest market share player. If that is you, chose the number two player. Your focus needs to be on collecting data that is related to the system performance parameters that make up the Value Metric for your particular product type and market segment. This will take some detective work, but it can be done. Specific actions you can take include:

- Analyze any papers, articles, or press releases for clues pointing to how and when your competitor will be making performance improvements.
- Research patent filings.
- Put your sales and service organization to work finding out what your competition is telling your customers about their plans.

With this information, try to re-create your competitor's product roadmap. Identify when new products will be introduced and how they will perform against your Value Metric.

Second, take a look at your segment's historical performance against your Value Metric. Try to get a feel for the average annual performance improvement that your industry segment has typically produced.

Now you're ready to create your Value Metric performance history and forecast plot like the one in figure 8. Just follow these four steps:

1. Plot the historical performance for the product's Value Metric minus the price parameter. For now you can ignore price. For

performance target setting, system price is assumed to be equal across all suppliers. Do this for your system and your benchmark competitor.

2. Extend the Value Metric line for your competitive benchmark based on your forecast for their future performance. Use an estimate based on historical trends to extend this line beyond where you have specific data points.
3. Extend a line from your product's current performance into the future so that it is always 25 percent greater than the competitive benchmark.
4. Mark the point on your product's line where you would like to introduce your new product. The Value Metric at this point is the minimum value for your new system's target performance.

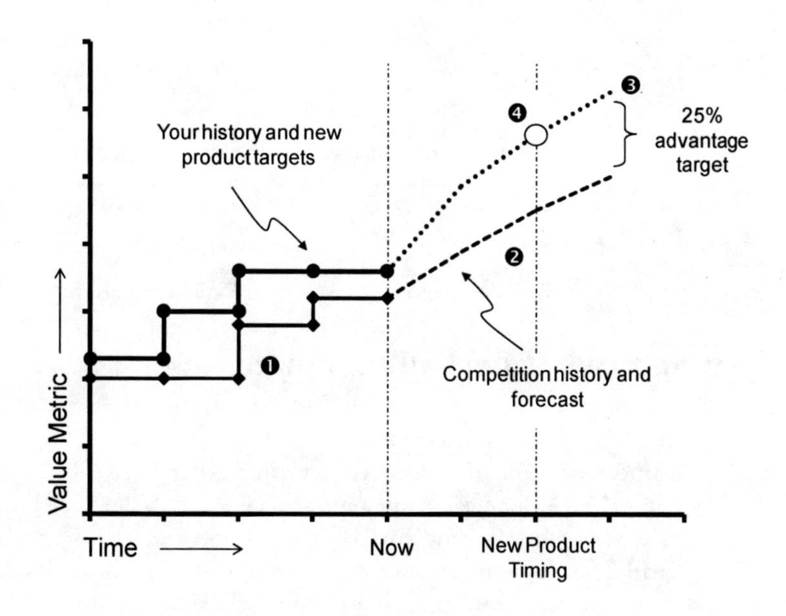

Figure 8: Value Metric History and Forecast Plot

There is one important point to remember about Value Metric usage when setting roadmap targets. Assume equal pricing among competitors and only plot product performance and operating cost attributes from the Value Metric for your product. The reason for this is that price is usually how an equipment supplier captures value for a performance advantage or makes up for a performance deficit. If you were to include price in your plots, you'd find that the line for you and the line for your competitor lie on top of each other.

Also, capital equipment markets tend to demand ever-increasing performance at near-constant pricing. This would create a horizontal plot over time.

Use the Value Metric to Estimate Market Pricing

To put a specific dollar value on your product, put your Value Metric expression, except for system price, on one side of an equal sign, and enter the data for your competition on the other as shown in figure 9. Then, solve the equation for your system price. The number you come up with is the approximate market value of your system.

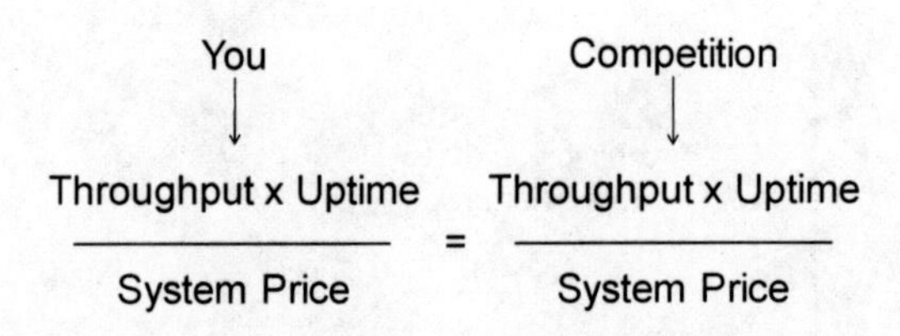

Figure 9: Value Metric Expression for Estimating Market Pricing

Communicate Value with Comparative Financials

The Value Metric concept is also used to communicate your value proposition. The most important element of a sales tool kit is a set of comparative financial statements showing the "value" of buying your product against buying that of the competition. This can be in the form of a profit or cost-savings comparison. The goal is to show the customer just how much more they will make or save by selecting your system over that of the competitor. When doing this, use a price for your product as high as you can while still showing a value advantage.

Working with our ion implanter example, suppose that your system has 25 percent higher throughout and 5 percent more uptime than your competitor's system has. Your comparative financials would look like those in the table 8.

Table 8: Example Comparative Financials

	You	**Competition**
Maximum System Throughput/Year	20,000,000	16,000,000
System Uptime %	90%	85%
Total Units Produced/Year	18,000,000	13,600,000
System Price	$4,500,000	$4,000,000
Depreciation Cost/Year	$900,000	$800,000
Depreciation Cost per Unit	$.050	$.059
Savings/Unit	$.009	
5 Year Savings	$810,000	

Notice that the only inputs to the table were the three primary selection criteria from the Value Metric:

- Throughput
- Uptime
- System price

With just these three elements, it was possible to create a simple set of financials to describe your system's value from the buyer's perspective. In this example, your system, even at a $500,000 price premium, will save the customer over $800,000 in the first five years. Assuming that you could back up these claims with data and demonstration results, you'd be on very firm ground when the time comes to justify your pricing during purchase negotiations.

Real Value Wins More Orders at Higher Prices

Technical features and advantages may contribute to the value of your product or service, but they are not value itself. Value is a financial expression. Knowing what it is and using it to drive your product and marketing strategy will enable you to show customers how they will make more money by buying your product. As a result, you will win more orders at higher prices.

7. Market Share Leads Gross Margin

I don't think there's a high-tech sales or marketing professional that hasn't argued, "We need to discount to break into this account, and once we're in, the gross margin will go up."

This is usually rebuffed by the general managers and finance people who argue, "If the product is as good as marketing says, then you just need to convince the customer of its value. We need to get our price. The market share will follow."

So, who's right?

Market Share Usually Comes First

You've got your marching orders to penetrate that key account. The competition has been entrenched for the last three years, but you're not deterred. You hit your customer with your best presentation, touting your advantages and the higher profits that they will realize as a result of your product's technological breakthrough. Point by point, it's clear that you're better than the incumbent.

Your solution looks great on paper, and even the product demonstration went well. But, the problem is that the only way the customer knows for sure your system will work is to buy it and use it. That's a lot of risk for your customer, especially if his existing solution is acceptable.

What you have to realize is that your customers have already invested a lot in optimizing the competitor's product. They've trained operators, optimized the process, and made a sizeable investment in spare parts. They even know your competitor's weaknesses and have figured out how to work around them.

There will be a cost associated with switching to your system. Your customers will have to re-learn everything and rebuild their support infrastructure. They'll assume you have weaknesses too, and expect that they'll have to relive the painful discovery process all over again. Switching to your system will initially be more expensive and less efficient for your customer even if your advantage claims hold up.

In order to overcome the customer's switching costs and risks, compromises on standard pricing and terms may be necessary when penetrating a new account. These concessions can take the form of a:

- Longer-than-standard warranty
- Applications support to qualify your system
- Risk-free evaluation period
- Period with the right to return the system
- Discount off the system price

As a result, that penetration deal often doesn't have the gross margin that you were looking for. Thus, in the case of high-tech capital equipment, market share usually comes first.

However, making concessions to break into an account doesn't automatically mean that higher gross margins will follow. Margins will only follow if your product provides a true value advantage.

Advantage Must Be Experienced for Margins to Follow

So you've broken into that key account, but you took it on the chin for that first order. That's okay, because better pricing is sure to follow, right? Not so fast. Your product must have a real, tangible value advantage over that of your competitor. If the advantage isn't clear, higher gross margins will not necessarily follow.

Your product positioning, data, and demonstration got you this far, but now your product is parked right next to that of your competitor. It's time for a real-world, head-to-head performance evaluation in your customer's environment. At this point, there's a big change in how your system will be evaluated. It's no longer your data that matters; it's theirs. It's no longer your demonstration results; it's their production results. Once your system lands on your customer's production floor, there is no faking it. It's here, in your customer's environment, running your customer's product that your system must demonstrate its advantage over the incumbent.

But having an advantage is only half the battle. Remember, the competitor's product is already integrated into your customer's process. The customer's staff is already trained, and their stock room is full of the competitor's spare parts. Your competitor's support infrastructure advantage also needs to be overcome. The deck is stacked against you.

That means that your support during the head-to-head evaluation phase needs to be impeccable, and you need to get the customer up the experience curve fast by focusing on:

- Solving issues with lightning speed.
- Making the customer experts on your product.
- Establishing regular communication.
- Defining success criteria and tracking performance.
- Getting spare and consumable parts logistics up and running.

It would be a tragedy to have a true advantage but fail to capitalize because the support wasn't in place to make sure that the customer was successful. Once the customer experiences your value advantage and has made an investment in your product's success, the door is open for margins to improve.

Structure Penetration Deals to Tee-Up Follow-On Pricing

When doing a penetration deal, you want to set the stage for follow-on orders, but don't negotiate them right away. There are two big mistakes that can doom you to a lifetime of penetration pricing.

The first mistake is trying to negotiate follow-on orders with the penetration deal. Before you've been qualified by the customer, you are in your worst negotiating position. They haven't experienced your value, and they haven't made a monetary, political, or emotional investment in you or your system. Negotiating a volume deal at this point almost assures the customer a fleet of systems at penetration pricing.

In addition, the terms will probably include an escape hatch for the customer, since she hasn't proven for herself that your system will work. So, in essence, you end up committed to multiple systems at compromised prices, while the customer really only committed to give your system a workout. Your position will improve once the customer has experienced success with your product. Wait until then to negotiate follow-on orders.

The second mistake is to fool yourself into thinking that you'll penetrate a capable competitor's account on standard pricing and terms. In this case, you stick to your guns on price and terms deep into the sales process because you cannot stand the thought of discounting or offering special terms until you absolutely have to.

However, when the purchasing manager threatens to stick with the incumbent at the last minute, there's a good chance panic will follow. Then it's all hands on deck to save the order. There's no time to think about how to preserve the concept of your system's value in order to protect future orders. You've got to get this order, and there's no time to recover, so you capitulate on price and terms. You've now trained the customer to expect a last minute cave-in, and all sense of the real value of your system has dissolved. The baseline for follow-on orders is now the penetration deal and pricing.

To help avoid this situation, create an official new customer package. Give it a name. This name doesn't even need to be creative. "New Customer Start-up Program" will work just fine. This program is a package of special pricing, terms, and support designed to compensate the new customer for the costs and risks associated with qualifying your system.

Get this program on the table right in the beginning of the sales process. This program should include supporting marketing materials to communicate the value that these special incentives have in helping new customers mitigate switching costs and risks. This will legitimize the offer as a one-time program for new customers rather than as a heat of the moment capitulation.

Throughout the sales cycle, keep standard terms and pricing visible and separate from any concessions to help mitigate the customer's switching costs and risks. New customer concessions should be explicitly called out as just that and always discussed in the context of your special start-up program. While not a panacea, this will at least help keep the starting point for future negotiations from being pegged to the original penetration deal.

Four Keys to Ensuring That Gross Margin Follows Market Share

Market share often precedes target gross margin performance because the supplier must share in the customer's switching costs and risks. The four keys to ensuring that gross margins follow after a penetration deal are:

1. Do not bundle follow-on orders with penetration deals.
2. Outline a penetration sales process and contract that sets expectations for follow-on pricing and terms.
3. Develop a robust support plan to get your customer up the experience curve.

4. Provide a real value advantage that your customer experiences in her environment.

8. Gaining Platform Leverage

A well-designed platform strategy is a surefire way for capital equipment suppliers to develop leverage, and in return, harvest large results from small efforts.

In high-tech capital equipment, a product platform is a collection of common elements that can be deployed across multiple products. When implemented correctly, a platform strategy can deliver significant competitive advantages in development speed, operating leverage, and profitability. [ii]

Why Is a Platform Strategy Critical?

Ever notice that some capital equipment companies seem to be able to develop and deploy new products and product improvements faster than others? Those same companies also tend to produce a steady stream of very profitable upgrades for their installed base. Look under the hood, and you are likely to find that an effective platform strategy is the engine driving this performance.

In terms of competitive advantage, a well-thought-out platform strategy can be more important than product strategy, because it:

- Enables new products to be deployed rapidly.
- Produces operating leverage.
- Creates a barrier to entry for your competitors.

New products can be deployed more quickly because you have a concentrated resource pool developing a platform that spins off multiple products. Only a fraction of the system requires unique development to create these individual products. This means that a small investment in engineering can produce a large product portfolio. With an effective platform strategy, you'll develop new products faster and cheaper than a competitor who develops every product from the ground up.

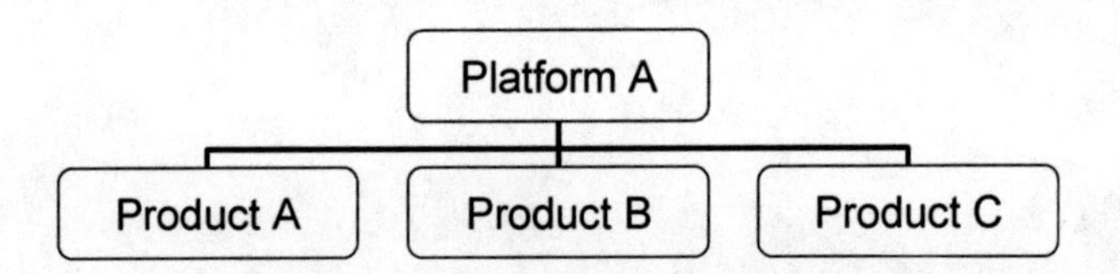

Figure 10: Platform with Multiple Derivative Products

Operating leverage also comes from platform commonality. In addition to product development leverage, an effective platform strategy can produce a high level of parts and module commonality across a platform's products. This means that your operation is managing fewer parts, buying in higher volume, and developing fewer manufacturing procedures. The leverage doesn't stop there. You will also have a more efficient field spares inventory as well as field service engineers who can be cross-trained across multiple products in a snap.

Finally, all of those benefits of operating leverage will help keep competitors out of your accounts. If customers buy multiple product types from your common platform, they will also experience the same operating efficiencies in their spare parts' management and service engineering cross-training. This increases the switching costs that a competitor must overcome to steal a piece of your business.

I think you can see that platform strategy is fundamental to creating competitive advantage and therefore should be a key focus for a company's senior management team.

Platform Strategy Example

Let's say you were a manufacturer of thin film deposition equipment for one of the semiconductor related industries. Your product would likely be made up of something like these basic building blocks:

1. Substrate handler
2. Vacuum system
3. Facilities module (process gas, water, power)
4. Control system
5. Process chamber
6. Deposition source

Suppose there are several applications for thin film deposition in your market, so you would likely end up with several products. That's good. It would be even better to be able to create and market each of these products by just making small tweaks to an overall platform.

But not all platforms are created equal. Platform strategy follows a continuum from just products (poor) to platforms that contain the elements that deliver your vector of differentiation (excellent).

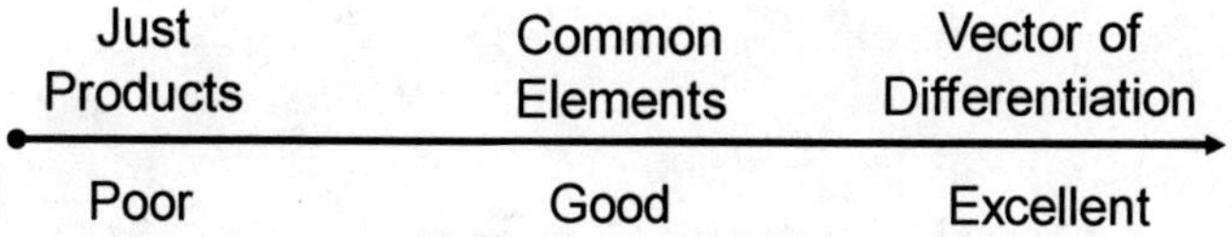

Just Products — Common Elements — Vector of Differentiation

Poor — Good — Excellent

Figure 11: Continuum of Platform Strategy Quality

Let's say that you were able to keep the wafer handler, vacuum systems, facilities module, and deposition source the same for all of your products, and all you needed to do was develop application-specific process chambers. In this scenario, you would have a set of common elements across multiple products, a "good" platform strategy.

At this level, your company would be able to rapidly deploy new products since:

- Creating new products only requires new development on a subset of platform elements.
- Product development on common elements is leveraged across all products.

Let's take this example one step further. Suppose the technology that delivers your competitive advantage is in the deposition source, and this source is common to all the products derived from the platform. Now your platform is not only a collection of common elements, but it also contains your vector of differentiation.

By having this vector of differentiation at the platform level, you are in position to invest at a rate much greater than if it resided at the product level. This accelerates your competitive advantage.

Think of it this way. If five products are derived from your platform, but the differentiating technology lives in the products not the platform, you'll need five R&D efforts to maintain your competitive advantage. However, if your vector of differentiation is contained within the platform, you only need one R&D effort. Since that R&D effort is leveraged over the revenue from five products, you're in a position to invest at two, three, even four times the rate of your competitors, thus improving the probability that you will sustain your competitive advantage.

What to Do with a Poor Platform

This platform strategy is pretty powerful stuff, but unfortunately we don't all get to start with a clean sheet of paper. What if you find yourself with a portfolio of products that should have been, but were not conceived as part of a comprehensive platform strategy? This often happens when the portfolio was assembled by merger and acquisition.

Chances are that you won't be able to achieve all of the leverage of an excellent platform strategy, but you can improve your situation.

Working with our example, this time let's assume that we have a portfolio of thin film deposition systems that do not have the common platform that they could have. The strategy would be to migrate toward commonality with each iteration of the product design. The basic steps are:

1. Define the platform scope (i.e. which products belong).
2. Define the elements or subsystems of the platform.
3. Identify the "golden elements" that you want the products to migrate to.
4. Track progress with a platform compliance roadmap for each product.

Golden elements are the best of the subsystems across the products in the scope of your platform. For example, let's say the substrate handler from a particular product is the best. Then you would want to migrate all of the products to adopt this handler, all else being equal.

You can keep the desire to achieve more platform leverage in front of your organization by including a platform compliance matrix as part of your product roadmap reviews. See figure 12 for a sample compliance matrix.

Platform Name		Product Line Name		
Element	Golden Element	Today	N+1	N+2
Substrate Handler				
Vacuum System				
Facilities Module				
Control System				
Process Chamber				
Deposition Source				

Figure 12: Platform Compliance Matrix

In the column labeled "golden element," you would place the name of the platform element that you desire all products to migrate toward. Then in the next three columns, you would indicate the degree of compliance (a percentage or a color code) for each product on your roadmap, starting with the current product.

The speed and degree with which you drive adoption of the golden elements across the product line will depend on factors such as:

- Expected life of the product
- Time and cost to integrate the designs
- Impact on installed base
- Expected return vs. other investments

Very rarely is a complete product line overhaul for a legacy platform problem practical. Redoing everything and staying competitive may be too risky and costly. But that doesn't mean that you can't make incremental steps in the direction of commonality to gain at least some of the leverage that effective platform strategy provides.

9. What to Do in a Downturn

Mismatches in supply and demand can easily occur in capital equipment markets, making them more subject to cyclical downturns than other industries. This is caused by the large lag times between demand recognition and new capacity implementation. Here's how the typical scenario plays out.

When global semiconductor manufacturers see an excess demand for memory chips, they place new equipment orders to expand capacity. The time between placing equipment orders and bringing the new capacity on line can be many months. The excess demand still appears to exist even though manufacturers have responded. So, manufacturers continue to place more orders for even more new equipment.

Eventually, this new manufacturing capacity will start to come on line. Since the timing of demand recognition and capacity implementation is skewed, new capacity usually overshoots the initial demand. This puts the brakes on new equipment purchases, and it even spurs attempts by late comers to cancel orders. A cyclical downturn ensues until the excess capacity is absorbed.

This is simply a part of life for capital equipment manufacturers. There are some key things that you can do to make sure that your company effectively manages these inevitable ups and downs.

Stay Focused

In a downturn, it will feel like your current strategy isn't working. The question for you is, "Is the downturn fundamental or cyclical?"

The "yo-yo and the staircase" metaphor works here. Imagine that you are watching a person walk up a staircase; at the same time he is playing with a yo-yo. The yo-yo represents industry cycles, and the staircase represents the fundamental industry direction.

There's no need to panic with the first sign of a downturn. If your current condition is cyclical, then the biggest mistake would be to respond with fundamental changes to your business. For example, if it didn't make much sense to get into the system refurbishment business when the yo-yo was at its peak, then it probably doesn't make sense when it's fully extended. Instead, ask yourself the following questions.

- Are your market assumptions and business goals still valid?
- Is your fundamental strategy sound?
- What is it about your offering that keeps customers coming back?
- What drives your long-term profitability?
- What are the strategic imperatives that must be preserved?
- What are the non-essentials that distract from the fundamental strategy that can be cut if necessary?

As a cyclical downturn lengthens, calls to change course will accelerate. Your discipline will be tested, but you need to resist. If you lose your focus, you run the danger of being overtaken by a competitor when conditions improve. Business will eventually return, if you manage to stay the course and prepare for the upturn. Additionally, you'll be stronger for it.

Engage Your Customers

It's a mistake to stop engaging with customers during a downturn, just because they aren't buying. During this time, there are two things that you must do to prepare your company for the eventual upturn.

The first is to stay close to your customers' technology roadmaps. Technology will continue to march on, even during a downturn. If you are not staying close to the changes that are occurring in your industry, you run the risk of missing an inflection point and finding yourself out of position. Use a downturn to get closer to your customers. Seek to develop a better understanding of your customers' problems and their options for solving them. Use this insight to gain advantage over a competitor who decided to weather the downturn by hiding in his office at company headquarters.

The second is to position your company to be ready for the initial stages of an upturn. When the upturn eventually comes, your customers will begin to purchase equipment again. The pattern of these initial purchases will depend on which of their markets recover first and on the ability of their current manufacturing equipment to address them. Key questions to ask your customers include:

- Which markets do you expect to recover first?
- How will that affect your manufacturing process?
- How will that affect the manufacturing equipment mix in your factories when the upturn comes?

Use this information to position your product portfolio and gain advantage when the market rebounds. You may gain insight into possible upgrades for your current installed base that will address the anticipated market requirements and possibly block your competitor. Or, you might also see an opportunity to make adjustments to product roadmap priorities to improve your position when things turn around.

In a downturn, don't withdraw from your customers just because the orders have temporarily dried up. The next upturn isn't likely to look like the last. If you're not fully engaged with your market, you'll have no way to figure out what is going to be different.

Prepare for Your Competitors' Moves

During a downturn, competitors will be more aggressive than ever in targeting your business. You need to think about what their moves are likely to be and plan your response. For the few systems orders still out there, you can expect your competition to attack with:

- Lower prices
- Aggressive performance commitments
- Extended payment terms

Think about how you will deal with these downturn realities to protect your market position and profitability. Don't do this in the heat of battle. Instead, anticipate it and have a game plan. Ask yourself questions like the following.

- Is there a way to link your installed base to new system orders such as a service or upgrade offering?
- Is there a way to reduce product costs, such as reducing features sets or specifications, to protect profitability in a period of weak pricing?
- Are there high-value, low-cost offerings that you can bring to the table such as extended warranty, training, or applications support to help in tough negotiations?

Protect Your Key Employees

The high-technology capital equipment business demands a unique skill set from its workforce. Think about it. Success requires an understanding of fundamental physics, chemistry, and material science, with an ability to apply that knowledge to design, produce, sell, and service equipment with multi-million-dollar price tags. It's an industry where PhD's are as common in marketing as they are in research and development. The best people in this industry are a rare and extremely valuable asset.

In a downturn, employees get discouraged and are vulnerable to overtures from your competitors. Make sure that you protect your key employees by creating special incentive plans that reward loyalty as well as performance. Make sure that these incentives are based on the realities of the business climate and are not unrealistic goals that will discourage your top performers.

In a downturn, costs must be cut to manage profitability and conserve cash. This requirement is often in conflict with trying to preserve the talent pool. Trying to avoid a reduction in force by implementing reduced work weeks, salary cuts, or suspending 401K matching isn't a magic bullet. Often this is done in the name of trying to save jobs. This is a noble cause, but it could push your best employees out the door.

Consider this. If a company sees its business fall off by 25 percent, it figures that it needs to cut headcount-related expenses by 20 percent to break even. Instead of having a 20 percent reduction in force, the company decides to put the remaining workforce on a four-day work week and suspend 401K matching.

What do you think the company's best employees are doing on their day off?

Chances are that the most valuable players will be looking to work for a company that can provide a full week's salary and a 401K match.

When it comes to downsizing, figure out what the headcount needs to be and get there as soon as possible. Try to focus reductions in those areas that are volume sensitive and relatively easy to rebuild. Do your best to stay away from those areas that are difficult to rebuild, such as areas in which work loads are relatively independent of the current business levels and projects are critical to maintaining competitive advantage.

Then, make sure those employees that remain have good reason to stay. You are going to need your best people, as they will form the foundation for strengthening your organization once the upturn does arrive.

10. Getting Disruptive Technology Right

Every once in a while, a market experiences the birth of a disruptive technology. Examples are all around. Take for example the telephone, the airplane, the Internet, and stealth weapon systems, to name a few.

As a capital equipment provider, you usually experience disruptive technology as a manufacturing process innovation that produces a step-function improvement in your customers' manufacturing process, cost of ownership, or product performance. For you, introducing such a disruptive technology can mean a jump in profit margins or a compelling competitive advantage.

Bringing a disruptive technology to market, however, is a complex, risky, and expensive undertaking especially for capital equipment suppliers. But, if executed well, breakthrough results are possible. To improve your chances of success, you need to follow these four rules for getting disruptive technology right.

1. Make sure there's a big problem.
2. Don't go it alone.
3. Get a statement of work.
4. Don't get ahead of yourself.

Make Sure There's a Big Problem

As ironic as it seems, buyers of high-technology capital equipment are usually very conservative.

Semiconductor manufacturers are a perfect example. Although we think of them as technology junkies, they actually will do everything in their power to extend existing methods just to avoid the risk of adopting a new technology. That's because new technology brings new risks. That's why a really big problem or tremendous opportunity must exist—one that your customers cannot address with their existing technology. Without this, their risk tolerance never rises to a level at which a disruptive technology will be seriously considered.

A really "big problem" in this sense is first and foremost "economic." Solving it means a windfall in profits for your customer. This can come in the form of a step-function improvement in competitive advantage, market opportunity, or cost reduction. If there's going to be risk, then there must be reward.

A really "big problem" is also pervasive. An isolated issue for one customer isn't a big problem in this sense. It's just an engineering project for you. While solving it may create disruptive value for one customer, you need a problem that's pervasive in your industry in order for you to justify the investment to solve it.

Don't Go It Alone

Probably the most important ingredient to a successful disruptive technology introduction is a committed customer partner.

You simply cannot get enough visibility into your customer's world on your own. In the world of high-technology capital equipment, your disruptive idea has a pretty good chance of requiring changes to your customer's up and down stream manufacturing processes. It's not likely to be a drop-in solution. Designing the other changes that are required in order to integrate your disruptive technology is beyond the capability of most equipment suppliers. Without the help of a customer partner, it's nearly impossible to get a handle on what's really required to turn a technology breakthrough into a successful product.

Engaging with customers to drive disruptive technology adoption is very different than trying to sell an existing product into an existing market. Make sure that your sales team understands that they are helping you identify partners, not prospects. The last thing you want is for your disruptive, "not-ready-for-prime-time" technology to show up on a request for quotation, leaving you in the awkward position of having to circle back and reset expectations.

Also, don't confuse customer partners with curious customers. New technologies generate a lot of interest, which can quickly translate into dozens of requests for follow-up presentations and demonstrations. If you're not careful, you can spend a lot of time and money satisfying the R&D community's technical curiosity and have nothing to show for it.

Not going it alone does not mean working with everybody. It means working with a very short list (sometimes just one) of the best customer partners that you can find. The best candidates are typically:

- Experiencing the big problem that you are trying to solve
- Willing to put skin in the game to help solve it (money, people, time, other resources)
- An industry leader that the rest of the market tends to follow
- A good cultural fit with your company
- Broadly supported in their own organization to pursue a partnership

Once you've developed your short list of customer partners, let sales know that engaging customers outside the list will be limited to status updates while you're developing and validating your new technology. This "closing of the gate" is a critical step to ensure that your program doesn't have to deal with unnecessary distractions.

Your diligence in selecting the right partner will also pay off as you fight the inertia to stick with incumbent methods. Through the course of your technology development and introduction program, there are going to be some dark moments when it seems like everyone wants to throw in the towel and go back to the way things were. Having a committed partner will be a big help in keeping the status quo at bay.

Get a Statement of Work

Nothing is more fundamental to the success of a disruptive technology partnership than a clear Statement of Work, or SOW. It defines how you and your partner will work together to develop the target technology and its application.

You are going to be working together for quite some time, so it makes sense to formalize this relationship and make sure that everyone is on the same page. The SOW will outline:

- Success criteria
- Deliverables
- Timelines
- Data sharing protocol
- Intellectual property handling
- Roles and responsibilities
- Process for modifying the SOW if necessary
- Terms for any equipment, test beds, or test devices that may be exchanged

The willingness of your partner to take this formal step is also a good litmus test for his commitment to do the work.

Don't Get Ahead of Yourself

When you start out, you'll have a new technology, but you won't have a market. If you don't have a market, you can't define a product. If you can't define a product, engineering can't make one. Be patient and don't drive yourself crazy trying to define the final product right out of the blocks. You have a few phases that you need to get through before you can do that. Figure 13 shows the three phases.

Phase	Investigation	Validation	Productization
Who	Potential Partners	Small List of Partners	Beta System Partners
What	Identify Market Potential	Validate Technology	Validate Production Worthiness
System Needed	Experimental Platform, Doesn't Ship	Shippable, Pre-production System	Production System

Figure 13: Disruptive Technology Introduction Phases

Initially, you'll just need an experimental, non-shippable platform to demonstrate your new technology to prospective partners, just to validate that it has the potential to solve a big market problem. This platform only needs to demonstrate the technology and nothing more. It never leaves your engineering lab.

If that phase proves successful, you may need a pre-production system to ship to one of your partners so that she can validate the new technology in her own environment. This system is a little more mature than your experimental platform, but it may still be far from the final product. Expect requirements to evolve significantly in this stage as you debug the technology and modify it for use in your customer's environment. It is not uncommon for systems shipped in this phase to be returned or scrapped.

It's not until after the validation phase is well underway that you'll begin to know enough to define that winning product for the broader market. You'll develop this product and then ship initial units to beta partners. These beta partners should be the same customers that worked with you to validate the technology.

Get through each of these phases, and you'll have successfully turned your disruptive technology into a profitable, winning product.

11. Acquisitions: How to Separate the Wheat from the Chaff

Acquisitions are pursued to satisfy the desire for quick and significant growth. However, the process can be difficult and time consuming. Often you'll have to screen dozens of acquisition prospects before a short list of high potentials emerge. The challenge is finding a way to do this effectively and quickly.

Comprehensive treatment of new business acquisition strategies is beyond the scope of this book. However, for scenarios in which a larger company is considering purchasing a much smaller company to add a new technology to an existing portfolio, you'll find that the following tips will help you to quickly separate the wheat from the chaff.

Know What You Want

It's going to be very difficult to select the best candidates unless you are crystal clear on your objectives. You should be able to describe what you want for each of these items.

- Business or technology type
- Business size
- Geographical location
- All or part of the business

With this acquisition profile in hand, you can start to develop your list of potential candidates.

Two Steps to Quickly Screen Prospects

Once you've done the strategic work to determine the capability that you'd like to add to your business portfolio, it's time to select potential acquisition targets. What you're looking for is the wheat, with wheat being candidates that are a good strategic fit with a willingness to partner.

What you want to discard quickly is the chaff. There are two kinds of prospects that belong in the chaff category:

1. Those that are a good fit, but not interested in partnering
2. Those that are just a bad fit.

Your goal is to quickly screen prospects and avoid investing a lot of time with those that don't have partner potential. However, sorting this out can take a lot of time, even when done well. Too often, even after multiple meetings with a prospect, it's difficult to get a handle on his potential as a good match.

Your primary research against your acquisition profile will produce a list of potential partners. This list is the launching point for your screening process.

Step one is a phone call to the company's senior executive to communicate your interest in exploring a partnership and gauge theirs. Your script for the call should contain, but not be limited to, the following:

1. Explain why a combination or partnership between the two companies could make sense.
2. Describe the range of potential partnerships (acquisition, joint venture, etc.) that you would consider.
3. Ask if this is something that they would be interested in exploring further.
4. Ask for a face-to-face meeting if there is interest.

This conversation is your first screen. If step three produces a "no," then it's on to the next prospect. By the way, sometimes in that first conversation, the answer to number three doesn't come right away. It may be met with an, "I'll get back to you." That works because the ball is in their court.

The above phone script is admittedly direct. It's important to be cordial and establish trust, but it's also important to figure out where things stand as quickly as possible.

Step two is to establish expectations for the face-to-face meeting. Shortly after the telephone screen, forward the agenda below to the prospect in a letter or e-mail communicating that this is the kind of information you'd like to exchange.

Agenda for First Face-to-Face Meeting:

I. Your Company

- Company overview
- Objective

II. Their Company

A. Markets

- Key market growth drivers
- Historical/Forecast total available market
- Market share trend

- Key customers

B. Products

- Technical overview
- Primary competitors
- Competitive position
- IP position
- Roadmap

C. Financials

- Financial history and forecasts
- Revenue breakdown by product
- Gross margins by product line
- Current balance sheet
- Ownership structure

D. Organization

- Current organization structure
- Headcount and headcount distribution
- Management and technical team profiles

E. Facilities

- Locations owned and leased
- Factory tour

You'll notice that the agenda starts with you providing your company overview. This is consistent with the "you have to give, to get" rule. You'll find that going first goes a long way in establishing trust and increasing the information flow.

This agenda may seem overly comprehensive for the first meeting. Companies that are truly interested in partnering, however, generally do a very good job preparing for it. Those that do not are probably not really interested in a partnership. Either way, after one meeting, you'll be fully armed to assess the opportunity and decide your next move.

If you are a seller and your suitors don't request an agenda like this, you should prepare as if they did. You'll impress your suitor with your professionalism and the respect that you've shown for their time. You'll be off to a good start.

Selecting Your Best Targets

To know whether a potential merger or acquisition will really work, you have to do your homework. You'll need to conduct detailed due diligence to verify the accuracy and completeness of each piece of data that was presented. Look at the meeting agenda again, and for each item ask yourself:

1. How can I get independent verification of this data?
2. What additional data do I need?

If you have trouble coming up with a list for additional data in number two above, have your due diligence team ask everyone they meet at the target company two questions:

1. What are your company's three biggest opportunities?
2. What are your company's three biggest problems?

Then, ask the same questions to their customers, suppliers, and competitors. Don't be surprised if the answers actually create a new set of questions. During due diligence, you can expect new themes to emerge that will likely change the scope of your investigation. Be flexible, and follow any line of investigation that you think will lead you to a better-informed decision about your acquisition candidate.

Once you complete your due diligence, it's time to decide whether or not to acquire the company by answering the following questions.

1. Does the acquisition candidate clearly meet your acquisition profile?
2. Does it clearly fit your growth strategy?
3. Can you integrate the company?
4. Are you paying a fair price?

If you can answer yes to all four, you have found the wheat.

12.Maximize Your Aftermarket Profits

It was King C. Gillette's idea to "give the razors away, but charge whatever traffic will bear for the blades." This became known as the "razors and blades business model."

While capital equipment providers cannot afford to give their systems away, their aftermarket business is a significant portion of their revenue and profit. For veteran capital equipment companies, it's not unusual for their installed base to produce 30 percent or more of total revenue and sometimes more than 50 percent of profits.

This is a very significant business and deserves as much attention, if not sometimes more, than the "systems" business. Think of every system put into the field as an annuity of revenue and profit that comes in the form of services, spare and consumable parts, and system upgrades. The prize for a top notch aftermarket business is substantial. The key is to understand the dynamics of the different sources of revenue and align your organization to capitalize on it.

Service Quality Determines the Break-Fix Annuity

High-technology capital equipment requires a substantial amount of care and feeding to keep products performing at optimal levels. When there is a breakdown, it requires fixing. This cycle of breaking and fixing is what creates the "break-fix" annuity for capital equipment suppliers. The components of the break-fix annuity include:

- Spare and consumable parts and parts contracts
- Service and service contracts

The break-fix portion of the aftermarket business can be summed up as all of those things that your customer pays for in order to keep the system running the way that it should. Your customers hate this. Their view is that they are paying you for your failures. As a result, they are highly motivated to reduce or avoid break-fix costs. They will:

- Seek second source parts suppliers.
- Refurbish instead of replace parts.
- Design and manufacture parts themselves.
- Skip preventative maintenance.
- Service their own equipment.
- Negotiate parts and service pricing along with system purchases.

The last bullet really puts a cap on the break-fix business. Sophisticated capital equipment buyers know that on-going support costs are significant in the overall equipment cost of ownership. They have learned to extract running cost commitments from suppliers during system purchase negotiations to lock down their total costs and keep you from taking any unfair advantage down the road.

These actions by your customers undermine your quest for profit from aftermarket parts and services. To combat these forces, you need to understand that this is a service business. In a service business, the keys to success are providing exceptional service quality and an exceptional service experience.

Lexus, Toyota's luxury car division, is an example of how this looks when it's working well for the original equipment manufacturer. A long time ago, Lexus not only decided that it would operate a profitable aftermarket service business, but also that it would create competitive advantage with it. They have succeeded. An oil change at a Lexus dealership runs about two times what it would cost at your local quick-lube franchise. Lexus gets the business because of its exceptional service levels and quality.

Lexus owners can schedule an oil change over the Internet. When they arrive at the dealership, they pull into a clean, covered garage. A personal service concierge greets them and writes up their service order. They are given a free loaner car. When the car is finished, their service concierge calls to let them know that they can drop off the loaner car and pick up their car whenever it's convenient. Not only is their oil change done, but their car has also been washed and vacuumed.

And customers keep coming back every 5,000 miles even though they have a plethora of options at a fraction of the price.

This strategy can work for capital equipment suppliers as well, but you have to understand the concepts of service quality and the exceptional service experience. It starts with quality. When your customers turn to you for aftermarket service and parts, they expect perfection. This is warranted. In the break-fix service world, your customers are depending on you to keep their systems operational so that they can keep their manufacturing lines running. Any failure on your part to deliver defect-free service can cost them millions of dollars. What you are really providing is peace of mind.

Unfortunately, there are a lot of ways in which you can fail, including:

- Defectives parts
- Wrong parts
- Parts out of stock
- Shipping damage
- Parts arriving late

- Repair or maintenance execution errors
- Slow help-line response
- Faulty recovery after maintenance
- Inaccurate invoicing

Any departure from defect-free service gives your customer a reason to seek lower cost alternatives. So the first step to developing a successful break-fix aftermarket business is to implement the processes and infrastructure that will ensure defect-free service delivery, which includes:

- A closed-loop quality assurance program to ensure defect-free parts.
- Extending the quality assurance program to include ordering and shipping processes.
- A closed-loop parts logistics system to ensure that the right parts are in the right place at the right time.
- Robust service engineer training and certification to ensure that maintenance and repair procedures are performed quickly and correctly.
- Effective call center infrastructure including clear escalation procedures to ensure timely response to customer support requests.

The second step to success in the break-fix aftermarket business is to deliver an exceptional service experience. Deliver more than is expected. Deliver more than low-cost rivals do. Be extraordinary.

This may be hard to get your mind around. After all, it's a big enough challenge just keeping complex capital equipment running, never mind trying to figure out how to make the service experience exceptional. There are, however, things that you can do.

- Train technical support personnel to send customers regular updates on open issues, even when there's no meaningful progress to report. Customers like to know that you haven't forgotten them.

- Develop and send a regular newsletter to all of your system users with "best practices" tips and product updates. Profile a customer in each issue to give him some recognition in his community. Encourage subscribers to contribute articles.
- Include with every service call a complimentary system audit. Submit a formal report with the audit results. The formal report helps communicate the extra value that you provided. Not only will your customer appreciate this free system audit, but it may create a follow-on revenue opportunity.
- Sponsor a users' group in which users can get together and trade best-known methods. Hold regular meetings. Consider a web-based user forum or blog as well. You'll create a sense of community among your customers and help develop loyalty for your brand.
- Create automatic ordering and stocking services for consumable parts. Make it so easy to do business with you that you remove the temptation to seek low-cost suppliers.
- Generate a formal service report for the customer every time service is performed. Meet with the customer to review the report and ensure that she is satisfied with the services performed.
- If a service requires that parts be returned, provide return packaging including pre-paid shipping.
- Pre-package maintenance kits including pre-sorted hardware and maintenance procedures. Your customers can buy nuts, bolts, or insulators cheaper elsewhere, but they can't get them kitted in grab-and-go packages for a specific maintenance procedure anywhere except from you.

Upgrades: The Holy Grail of Aftermarket Profits

Different from the break-fix business in which customers are paying you to keep the systems running per their original specifications, the upgrades business is one in which they pay you to make the systems do more than they were originally capable of doing. While customers hate paying for break-fix services, they will jump at an opportunity to extend the capability of the systems they have already purchased, because it helps them extend the life of their capital investment, resulting in lower costs and more profit.

This creates one of the best profit opportunities for capital equipment manufacturers. This business has all of the elements of a perfect business.

- Built-in demand
- No competition
- Value-based pricing

Your customers are highly motivated to extend capital life. For many types of capital equipment, acquisition cost is the single biggest element related to cost of ownership. Your customers want to avoid having to purchase new equipment as long as possible. Anytime they can extend their existing installed base of equipment to the next generation technology or improve its productivity is an opportunity to avoid another round of acquisition costs. Sometimes it goes to the extreme in that customers demand to see upgrade roadmaps before they will make their initial system purchase. It's that important to them to ensure long capital life. This creates a "built-in demand" for system upgrades.

The best part is that the original equipment manufacturer (OEM) is almost always the only one who can provide these upgrades. Upgrading the productivity or technical capability of complex equipment requires a complete knowledge of the system hardware, control system, and software. It is almost impossible for a third party to gain control of this business. For the OEM, this is a virtually competitor-free environment.

This sets up the opportunity to price upgrades based on the value provided. Let's say that your upgrade enabled an existing system to be used for a next generation manufacturing process. Without this upgrade, your customer would have to buy all new equipment. Your value is that you helped the customer avoid new system acquisition costs. It's pretty likely your upgrade product will cost you orders of magnitude less than the cost of a whole system to produce. And without competition to drive pricing down to minimum acceptable margins, you're in a position to achieve pricing anchored to the actual value provided.

Creating a successful business, however, requires some forethought. Products must be planned and developed with the upgrades business in mind. It is very difficult to generate a meaningful upgrades revenue stream as an afterthought. Products that generate a successful upgrades business typically have the following attributes:

- Products are derived from a common, multi-generation platform.
- Installed base upgrades are planned with each new product generation.

The aftermarket upgrades business is another reason why a robust platform strategy is essential to a capital equipment company's success. A common platform that survives multiple generations of new products facilitates backward compatibility. This means that capabilities developed with new products can easily be packaged into upgrades for the installed base. The longer the platform survives, the larger the upgrades revenue stream. That alone, however doesn't ensure success.

The organization must have the discipline to make sure that each new product development program also makes some or all of the new performance capability available as upgrades for the installed base. Designing new capability into a new product is almost always easier if it is not constrained with backward compatibility. The easy way out is to remove the constraint; however, this forfeits the upgrades revenue stream.

To make sure that your organization is making a robust trade-off decision between reducing design constraints and the upgrades business opportunity, force a return on investment review for the potential upgrade including:

- Incremental effort and risk of including backward compatibility as a requirement
- The value that the installed base upgrade would have to your customer

- Target pricing
- The cost of goods sold for the upgrade
- Total available market for the upgrade and expected revenue capture
- Total potential profit

The companies with the most successful upgrades business tend to treat the strategy and product development for installed base upgrades with the same rigor as they do their systems product lines.

Don't Let Aftermarket Be an Afterthought

Despite being such a big part of the overall revenue and profit engine for capital equipment companies, the aftermarket business is often treated as an afterthought. Symptoms of this include:

- Management reviews include system product lines but don't include service and upgrade products.
- Systems product lines have defined roadmaps and strategies but aftermarket product and service lines do not.
- Responsibility for the aftermarket business reports lower in the organization than other product lines.
- Systems product roadmaps do not include planned upgrades for the installed base.
- Systems product lines are managed by expert product and marketing managers but the aftermarket products are not.

The last bullet deserves a little more discussion. Often, the aftermarket business will get assigned to the customer service vice president. But, in capital equipment companies, service executives are typically hired because they are fantastic at executing the customer service function. They excel at managing large organizations, moving spare parts, installing systems, and controlling complex cost centers.

The attributes that likely won the service vice president her post are not the same ones that you need to develop your aftermarket business. For that you need the skills to evaluate opportunities and generate demand. While the customer service chief will likely know your customers very well, assigning aftermarket business development to her is generally a bad idea. Her skills and functional frame of reference are just not a match for the job.

The attributes that you're looking for are more likely to be found in your marketing vice president. Try dedicating a product manager in your marketing organization to aftermarket products and services, just like you do for systems. This is good move for two reasons.

First, you'll hire a business development and marketing professional with skills that match the task at hand. Moreover, this dedicated product manager will be under the tutelage of your marketing vice president. Second, the real aftermarket money, as discussed earlier, is made from installed base upgrades. This requires integrated planning with "systems" product roadmaps. There's a much better chance of a coordinated systems and upgrades strategy when both are part of the same marketing organization.

Aftermarket Value Pricing—A True Story

Less than one month into an assignment for a capital equipment company, I learned that an upgrade to increase system throughput was about to be launched through the service organization.

I met with the service executive in charge of the launch, who told me:

- 500 fielded systems were eligible for the upgrade.
- The original systems were sold for over $2M each.
- The upgrade improves system throughput by >25 percent.
- The upgrade cost of goods sold is ~$25K.

"Wow, sounds like a gold mine. How much are we selling the upgrade for?" I asked.

The service leader replied, "To hit my budget this year, I need to get 50 percent gross margin. So the price is $50K."

"Hmmm," I said, "from what you've told me, I'd bet this is worth in the neighborhood of $200K to our customers."

"Oh, don't go messing with my pricing. I know what I'm doing. Remember, this thing only costs $25K. I'm happy with a $50K price and so is my boss."

If my hunch was right, they were about to leave a ton of money on the table. So I went back to my office and sent an e-mail to the company's head of sales, describing the upgrade and asking how much he thought we could get for it.

He wrote back, "Most of the factories housing the upgradeable systems are completely filled. They are four-wall constrained, so expanding by adding new systems is not an option. The way I see it, every four upgrades is like getting a new $2M system without having to expand the facility. I suggest that we list at $250K and expect to realize an average of $200K."

I had a little fence mending to do with the service executive for coloring outside the lines, but in the end, the company upgraded over 200 systems at an average price of $190K.

The moral of the story is to make sure that your aftermarket business is in the hands of someone who thinks in terms of creating and capturing customer value, and not just internal budgets and product costs.

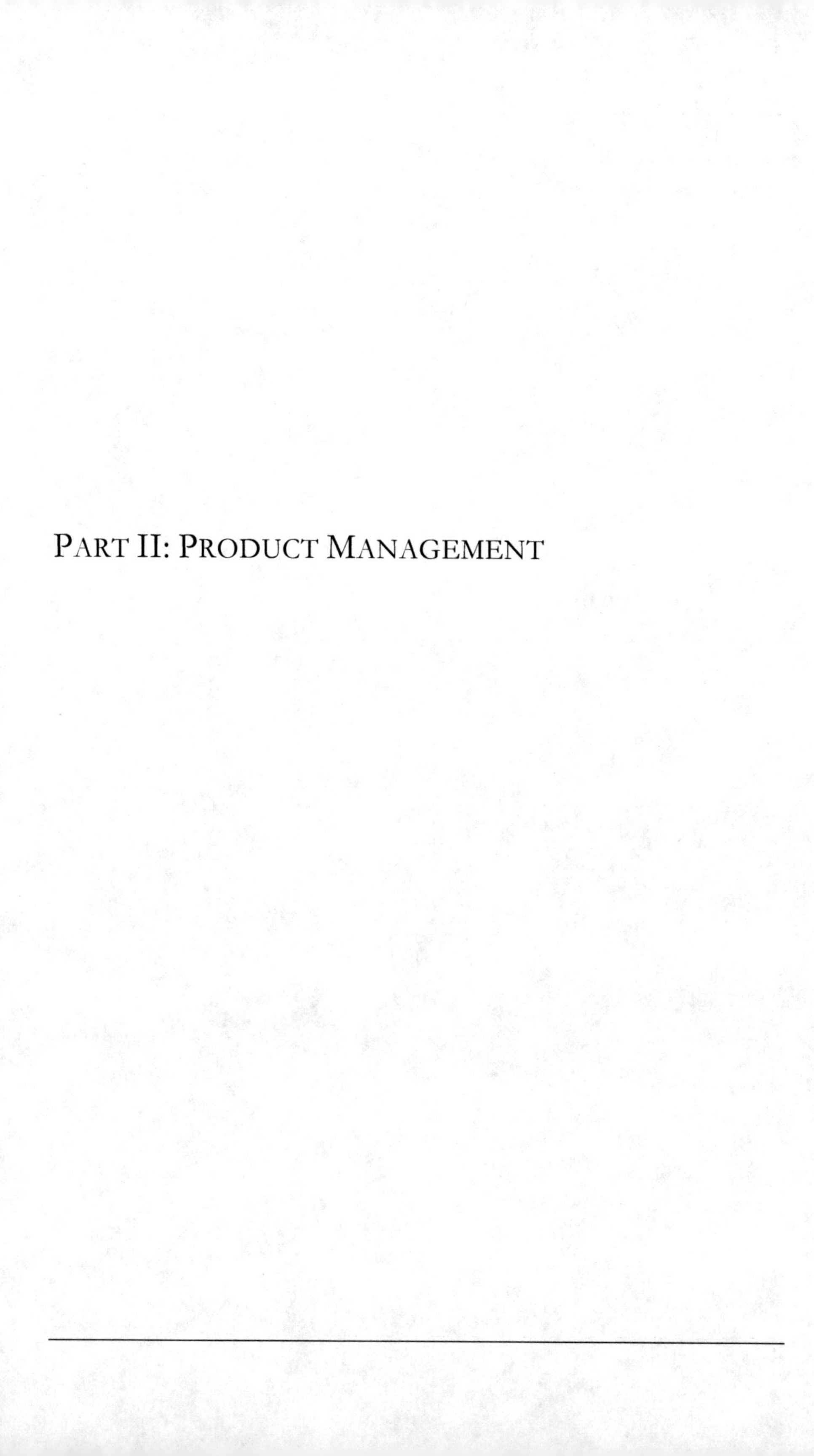

Part II: Product Management

1. Capital Equipment's Product Management Challenges

Capital equipment is all about outstanding products. It doesn't matter how skilled your sales team is or how efficient your operation runs; you're not going to climb to the top without your product management team turning out winning products. However, product management is not easy, especially for high-technology capital equipment companies.

Why It's So Difficult

Every company has the challenge of identifying a market, quantifying the opportunity, and then defining and implementing a solution to capitalize on it. Every company also has competitors breathing down its neck. But in capital equipment, product management is particularly difficult for the following five reasons.

1. High-technology capital equipment can take years to develop.

   A lot can happen between the time that you start and finish product development. Technology is constantly evolving, and competitors can change. Most likely, when you start a new development program, you'll find yourself asking customers questions about their requirements that they cannot answer. They just haven't figured out what they'll need two years down the road. As a result, you almost always have to start development long before customers even know what they need. It's almost guaranteed that the definition of the product will evolve during its development program.

2. High-technology capital equipment is complex.

   Often fundamental physics, materials science, and chemistry must come together in a package of sophisticated control and mechanical systems. Products can have dozens of subsystems and thousands of parts. Getting all of these components to work together is difficult, and they almost never work perfectly the first time.

3. The development teams are complex.

   It takes large cross-functional teams to successfully develop and introduce a new product. Scientists, engineers, marketers, suppliers, and more all have to work together. Just to add another layer of complexity, these teams may also be geographically dispersed. It's easy for entropy to prevail.

4. Everyone wants to be special.

   Capital equipment customers often use your gear to deliver their unique value. So, it's not surprising that they also want their equipment to be unique. This generates requirements for custom features, which in turn leads to complexities in product structure, configuration management, pricing, and after-sales support.

5. Great product managers don't just drop out of the sky.

   The complexities of managing high-tech capital equipment products set the qualification bar pretty high for the product manager. The really good ones are adept at working through technical, marketing, sales, customer support, and business issues. They understand the market, the technology, and the product. On top of that, they also have to be great leaders. They are rare and talented individuals.

And as if this isn't hard enough, when you finally do find the great ones, they quickly become the organization's "go to" product expert. Everybody wants a piece of them for engineering, sales, and service support, leaving them little time for actual product management.

Make Product Management a Core Competency

Making great capital equipment products is hard but not impossible. However, to be successful, you have to make a conscious decision to fully embrace product management as a formal discipline for planning, developing, and marketing products. The challenge is just too difficult and the task too complex to address in a casual manner.

Product management is everything from the planning, development, marketing, and support of a product. It's making the right product, the right way, at the right time. It's the systematic business process by which your company drives the commercial success of its products.

There are four key steps to establishing a product management core competency.

1. Develop first rate product managers who are influential members of the management team and have clearly defined roles.
2. Plan products via formal strategic planning, product roadmaps, and market requirements development.
3. Adopt and follow a product lifecycle management process.
4. Implement robust management controls to track and ensure product-line performance.

Establish the Product Manager Role

Step one to embracing product management is establishing the critical role of the product manager. The product manager has overall responsibility for the commercial success of the product or product line and manages the entire product life cycle.

This is a big job, one that frankly is often not fully understood and is under-appreciated by capital equipment companies. Staffing it with a junior person or burying it in the organization are common mistakes. This position can be described as the CEO of the product. If the role doesn't feel that big at your company, then you may want to take a second look at your approach.

Strategically, the product manager is the messenger of the market, making sure that decisions align with market needs and out-maneuver the competition. Tactically, he or she makes day-to-day trade-off decisions and drives the operational actions needed to ensure that the product meets its objectives. The product manager's role includes:

- Defining new products
- Determining market requirements
- Ensuring competitive advantage
- Creating product roadmaps
- Managing the Product Life Cycle (PLC) process
- Positioning products in the market and developing selling capability

Sometimes, the role of the product manager gets confused with that of program managers or product marketing managers. Each is a full-time job. The program manager manages product development while the product marketing manager drives all outbound product positioning and promotion plus sales force development. Except in the smallest of organizations, it's a mistake to ask any one person to fill more than one of these roles. It's like asking the CEO to also be the engineering vice president.

Figure 14 shows how each role relates to the three key activities in product management. Notice that only the product manager is concerned with product planning. If your company is like most, the bulk of your organization is consumed with making quarterly numbers, preparing for product demonstrations, or solving daily field issues. Product management is primarily a strategic role, but if the product manager is routinely consumed with daily issues like everybody else, you'll have nobody planning for the future.

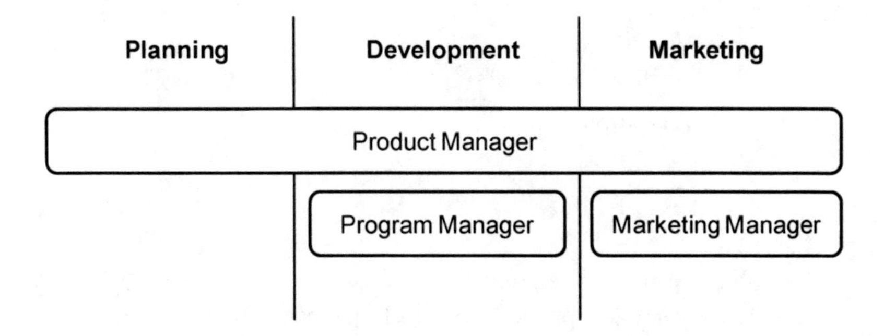

Figure 14: Key Product Management Roles vs. Activity

Formally Plan Your Products

Product planning is a formal, on-going process in which product managers make sure that the company is making the right products. It defines the overall product strategy and the selection of development programs. Product planning is all about:

- Selecting and defining target markets.
- Gathering customer requirements in order to align product strategy to customer technology roadmaps and application needs.
- Developing a competitive strategy and unique value proposition.
- Creating product roadmaps and detailed market requirements.

Probably the most important aspect of product planning is remembering to constantly validate and re-validate assumptions about market needs and the competitive environment, then adjust product plans as required. High-technology markets are very dynamic, and changes usually don't fit neatly into your annual planning cycle. Your ear must always be to the rail.

Adopt a Product Life Cycle Management Process

A Product Life Cycle Management or PLC process defines how all aspects of a product's life are managed from cradle to grave. A PLC process defines each major phase of a product's life.

1. Definition

2. Design
3. Verification
4. Validation
5. Production
6. End of Life

Each phase has a checklist of cross-functional deliverables due at the close of each phase. Most PLC processes establish decision "gates" between each major phase of a product's life where management determines whether or not the product team has met the requirements for passing onto the next phase.

Just about every established capital equipment company has some flavor of a PLC process in practice or sitting on a shelf. If you don't, then get one. However, failures in PLC management usually are not tied to the lack of a good process; they are usually related to a failure to follow it.

Assuming that you have a process, here are three things you can do to get your organization to develop rigor around a PLC process.

1. Train the players.

   This means product teams and management. You cannot follow or reinforce the process if the organization doesn't know it.

2. Walk the talk.

   If management isn't following the process or is constantly going around it with "exceptions," the discipline will never develop.

3. Change it if necessary.

   Not every detail of an "out-of-the-box" PLC process will work for your company. Forcing an element of the process that isn't working creates motivation to go around it. It's acceptable to make changes; just be sure to institutionalize them as revisions to the process.

Implement a Product Management and Control System

Management and control systems are the mechanism for assessing progress toward objectives, identifying risks, and establishing corrective actions. The secret to a good system is to ask the right questions and to be persistent and consistent about asking them.

Product-line performance management is no different. This can be accomplished with three key checkpoints or "reviews."

1. Product-line
2. Program
3. Phase gate

The purpose of the product line review is to assess overall product-line performance. These reviews are held on a regular basis, often quarterly. At this review, the product manager reviews product-line performance for senior management. The scope of this review includes:

- Scorecard metrics
- Financials
- Market position
- Product roadmap
- Product development
- Customer satisfaction

The purpose of this program review is to assess product development programs. It is also held on a regular basis, perhaps monthly. In this review, the product development program manager reviews program status with senior management. The scope of this review includes:

- Milestones
- Status vs. success criteria
- PLC deliverables status

- Product cost status
- Top issues and action plans
- Previous month's accomplishments
- Next month's goals
- Supporting data

A special review, called a phase gate review, is held whenever a program manager is ready to seek approval to move the program from one phase to the next in the PLC process. For example, a development program may be moving from the design phase to the verification phase. These reviews are not calendar driven, but event driven. Again, they are hosted by the program manager. The agenda is set to match the checklist of deliverables due for the phase being reviewed.

Product Line Review	Program Review	Phase Gate Review
Scorecard Metrics	Milestones	Phase Deliverables Review
Financial Performance	Status vs. Success Criteria	Phase Gate Decision
Market Position	PLC Deliverables Status	
Product Roadmap	Cost Status	
Product Development	Top Issue and Action Plan	
Customer Satisfaction	Last Month's Successes	
	Next Month's Goals	
	Supporting Data	

Figure 15: Three Reviews for Product Management and Control

When designing all of these reviews, create and use standard templates. Templates are a way of making sure that the right questions are being asked. Also as people get used to seeing data presented in a consistent manner, they spend less time trying to figure out what they are looking at and more time evaluating content. Your reviews will become more productive.

Be consistent with product-line and program review schedules. Set a regular schedule and stick to it. Probably the most valuable aspect of these reviews is that they force product and program managers to regularly get organized and assess their situation. They serve the same function as a board meeting for a CEO.

Finally, in all of these reviews, don't be satisfied with status reports only. Require that review owners articulate top issues and the actions required to address them. By doing this, you are helping them to clear out the daily mind-clutter and identify where they should spend their time. Try putting a slide in the presentation template titled, "Top Three Management Issues and Actions." If they get it right, you'll know that they have the big picture perspective needed to guide their product or program.

2. Habits of the Successful Product Manager

While it takes a team to design, build, test, and market capital equipment, there is one person that is absolutely crucial to producing a good product: the product manager.

The product manager position is a critical, difficult job that few do well. Product managers are responsible for all of the strategic and tactical activities that define a product and establish it in the market. They get all of the responsibility but none of the authority. They almost never get a staff. They're the first one called when the product has a problem, and they seldom get recognized when it's successful.

You'd have to be crazy to take a job like that!

The people who do are a rare breed, and finding or developing such people is hard. Good product managers are confident experts on their customers, competitors, and products. They don't thrive on organizational power; instead, they are obsessed with creating products that deliver superior value to the market.

Because of the unique challenges in capital equipment, product managers who do this well are highly sought after. And the best and brightest product managers always follow these six guidelines. They:

1. Get out of the factory
2. Always ask "why" to specify "what"
3. Communicate early and often
4. Understand the consequences of "Yes"
5. Always lead without authority
6. Link everything to money

If you want to rise to the top as a capital equipment product manager, or if you want to make sure that your organization develops them, then you'll strive to develop these behaviors. Let's investigate each.

Get Out of the Factory

Product managers who spend most of their time in the factory become very product centric and develop an "inside-out," rather than "outside-in" perspective on their products. That's the opposite of what you want in your product manager.

The best product managers view the world through the eyes of their market. They get out of the factory to learn about their customers, competitors, and the market dynamics that drive their business. But don't think for a minute that it's sufficient to only get out of the factory to support sales or service calls. More needs to be done, including the following:

- Attend customer technology reviews
- Meet with industry analysts
- Talk to past employees of competitors
- Attend conferences and trade shows
- Conduct roadmap reviews with customers
- Create and attend user group meetings
- Meet with suppliers

- Meet with players in adjacent markets
- Join and participate in industry groups

If product managers are supposed to be messengers of the market, they need to spend time in it. They need to get out of the factory and become an organization's most credible market expert.

Ask "Why" to Specify "What"

A product manager's most important function is to figure out what the product should be by figuring out the answers to the key "what" questions.

- What problem are we trying to solve?
- What market are we solving it for?
- What return can we expect when we solve it?
- What is our vision for beating the competition?

To develop the deep understanding of your customer that's required to get the "what" questions answered correctly, you need to ask "why." Whenever a customer tells you about a problem, ask them why it's a problem. Keep asking why until you fully understand the problem and its implications to your customer's business. You'll know that you've hit the core problem when the customer relates it to safety of people or product or to profit.

Also, don't get thrown when customers start requesting features. These are not requirements; they're solutions. If you're being asked for features, fall back on asking why until you understand the problem that they are trying to solve. As a product manager, you are not in the business of specifying solutions; you are in the business of specifying the market problems that are worth solving.

The detailed answers to the "what" questions end up in your Market Requirements Document (MRD) with things such as:

- What performance specifications

- What cost
- What price
- What time

The answers to the "what" questions spell out the requirements for a new product. If you've done your job well, you should be able to answer "why" for each and every one them.

Communicate Early and Often

As the product manager, you are likely the only one in the organization who is fully up to speed on all of the factors that affect your product's performance. You have the information that everyone in your organization wants and needs to know. It's easy, however, to forget about communicating, and it can be burdensome to put the information together unless you have a system.

Let's take a look at a typical product-line review agenda.

- Scorecard metrics
- Financials
- Market position
- Product roadmap
- Product development
- Customer satisfaction

This outline represents all of the information that you need to have at your fingertips and communicate to the organization. The best product managers carry around a standard set of slides with the latest status on all of the items. They keep them up-to-date by making sure that supporting organizations have a systematic way to maintain and report the data for their area of responsibility.

Now that we have an outline of "what" product managers need to communicate, let's tackle the concept of communicating early and often. Communicating early is important when something has changed that will have a major impact on the product. These changes can include:

- A major change to product development schedules
- A new market requirement that changes a development program's scope
- A major move by a competitor that effects product positioning
- A major product cost or development budget overrun
- The discovery of a major product defect

You need to communicate these changes early because usually the entire product team needs to adjust. Failure to communicate early can result in wasted effort going in the wrong direction or, even worse, bad decisions being made because no one was aware that things had changed.

As a product manager, you won't get away with just communicating a major change. You also have to lead the effort to figure out what to do about it. Always have options, a plan, and/or a recommendation for dealing with the change that you're communicating.

"Often" refers to the need to regularly communicate the big picture to the product stakeholders. As product manager, you may be the only one in the organization that can see the big picture, and you must share it regularly. You cannot possibly have the bandwidth to make every decision, so sharing the big picture with others gives them the context to make decisions that are consistent with the overall product direction even if you are not there. If you don't regularly provide the necessary information, day-to-day decisions will be based only on a narrow perspective of an issue.

A regular product-line review presented to your management serves as part of this communication, but not all of it. Not everyone does or should go to a product-line review, so you'll need to establish a few other mechanisms to get the word out. Here are some ideas for making sure that you are communicating the big picture often.

- Hold product update meetings with the product team. Present an appropriate version of the product-line review.

- In between product-line reviews, send regular product-line performance snapshots to management to keep them informed.
- When you go in the field, set aside time to provide a product update to the local sales and service teams.
- Have an elevator pitch for your product's top priorities and repeat them any chance you get.
- Carry around a hard copy of your product-line review or have it ready to go on your laptop. Use it as a visual aid whenever you're discussing product performance, status, or priorities.
- When you are in someone else's office discussing the product, illustrate your point on their white board. It will still be there long after you leave.
- Start and maintain an internal blog so that everyone can get and share the latest information whenever they need it.

Understand the Consequences of "Yes"

Everyone understands the consequences of "no." If you say "no" to whatever is being asked, then whatever that thing is doesn't get done. Say for example, you were asked if a special feature can be implemented in order to satisfy a customer request. A "no" means that the feature won't get implemented, and you'll potentially have a dissatisfied customer on your hands. That's easy enough.

It's not so easy to understand the consequences of saying "yes." However, most successful product managers do.

Understanding the consequences of "yes" begins with understanding the work triangle. The work triangle describes the interaction of scope, resources, and time for any task or project. The geometry of a triangle dictates that you cannot change any of its sides without affecting at least one other. The same goes for the work triangle shown in the figure 16.

Applying this to our example, implementing that special feature (an increase in scope), would require some combination of:

- Increasing the time for existing commitments

- Increasing resources
- Reducing the existing scope to accommodate the new feature

In order to maintain a handle on the consequences of saying "yes," you have to have your product line in control. That means having an understanding of the scope, schedule, and resources already committed to new product development and customer demands.

While it is always appropriate to look for opportunities to do more with less by optimizing plans and resources, good product managers know that eventually something has to give.

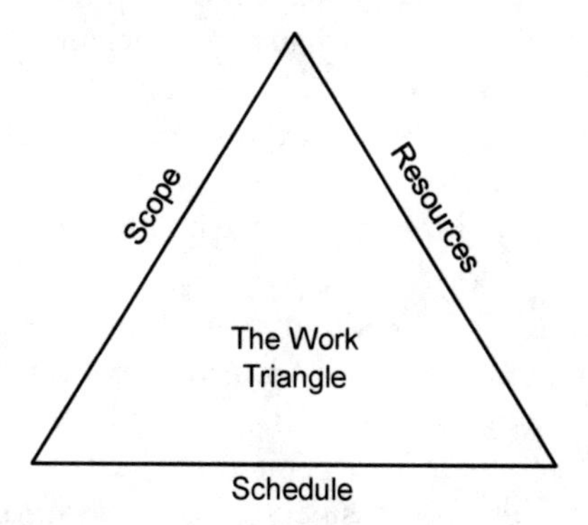

Figure 16: The Work Triangle

Lead without Authority

How do you galvanize your colleagues to follow when you've got all of the responsibility but none of the authority? The answer lies in your ability to articulate the win, exceed team members' expectations, and share the limelight.

If people don't know where you're headed, they can't possibly know "what's in it for them" when they get there. As a product manager, the most important thing that you can do is to articulate "the win" in simple, easy to understand terms.

The team needs to understand the value that the product or project will bring to the company. It could be such things as increased profitability, lower costs, or improved competitiveness. It's the product manager's job to connect the dots. Compare the following two objective statements for the same project.

1. "Our objective is to find and acquire a key technology."
2. "Our objective is to find and acquire a key technology to create a 40 percent performance advantage over our competition, resulting in dramatic market share and pricing improvement."

The first statement just describes the task. In marketing parlance, it's all about the feature, not the benefit. No value is equated to the win, so don't expect the masses to support your cause. The second statement, on the other hand, connects the dots between the task and the win. It appeals to our competitive instinct and desire to work on something important. Surely a project that has a direct impact on pricing and market share is going to have high visibility; therefore, it will rouse a desire to get on the bandwagon early and stay there.

Articulating the win doesn't only help the product manager inspire the team; it also cements sponsorship from senior management. Two good things will happen. First, you'll be less likely to fall victim to the budget axe when management understands the relationship between your product and business results. Second, management will echo your project's value, and your team will hear them validating that they are indeed part of something special and important.

The next key element to leading without authority is exceeding your team's expectations.

Imagine a scenario in which you're the product manager responsible for developing and launching a new system, and the project is in the very early stages of design. All of a sudden, you need the program manager to project materials costs for an executive review. You say, "Jim, we've got a product-line review Friday, so could you please put together a materials cost projection for the new system?"

That would be "meeting expectations" instead of exceeding expectations. What if you said: "Jim, we've got a product-line review Friday, so could you please put together a materials cost projection for the new system? I know you're really busy, so I brought you the bill of materials from last year's model with all of the cost information. I figured that would give you a head start."

That's exceeding expectations. Jim expects you to assign work, but he doesn't expect you to make it easy for him. Jim is more inclined to follow your lead when he sees that you are committed to going the extra mile.

Notice that we're talking here about exceeding team member expectations, not management expectations. Both are important, but exceeding management expectations results in getting assigned highly visible and important projects. It's exceeding team member expectations that results in an enhanced ability to lead.

Finally, learn to share the limelight. If you are the only person on the team that gets to report results, and you are the one always doing the talking, you can be sure that there will be some grumbling in the ranks.

One of the biggest human motivators is recognition. This means real recognition, not just mentioning and thanking the team before you present all of the project's achievements. Let team members present their own work to management, customers, and investors whenever you can.

Don't worry about missing out on recognition yourself, especially if you've been working on exceeding your team members' expectations. You'll find team members publicly crediting part of their success to your leadership, which is probably the best form of recognition.

Running a product line as a matrix manager can be one of the toughest management assignments. Without direct authority over the team, your only option is to create an environment that motivates the team to follow.

Link It All to Money

Successful product managers know that they are measured on the commercial success of their product line. Commercial success of a product is measured by the amount of revenue and profit that it brings to the company. It's all about the money.

Therefore, the best product managers link every business decision to saving money or making money. This means:

- MRDs don't just describe product features; they articulate the financial returns for achieving them.
- Product value propositions outline how much money the customer will make or save as a result of buying the product.
- Requests for additional resources are always coupled with the financial return for providing them.
- Priority trade-off decisions compare the financial outcome of the alternatives.

To get everyone's attention and ensure that you are working toward the commercial success of your product, link everything that you do to making or saving money.

3. Keeping New Product Development under Control

Did you ever sit through a two-hour product development review and afterward say to yourself, "I really don't know where this product stands. Is it going well? Are we behind schedule or ahead? Are we meeting our customers' expectations? Are we under budget or over?"

You're not alone.

Often, new product development reporting is jam packed with design concepts and drawings, with a few test results sprinkled in. This information is useful background, but it doesn't provide sufficient insight to the probability of success or when it might happen.

As a capital equipment executive, you live and die by the success of your new product development pipeline. What you're really after is a system of consistent, regular reporting across product development programs that will alert you to issues dealing with:

1. Product launch dates

2. Product performance
3. Product costs
4. Development costs

A consistent, concise, and precise approach to program reviews is required to ensure that program issues are quickly escalated to senior management for speedy resolution.

Program vs. Phase Gate Reviews

Since complex capital equipment products often have very long development cycles, a program can be in a single phase of your phase-gate development process for several months, even years. Control of these programs cannot be maintained with senior management phase-gate reviews alone. The time between reviews is just too long to prevent program entropy. What you need is a regular heartbeat of program reviews.

The phase-gate reviews occur upon phase-gate exits to seek management approval to proceed to the next phase. In these reviews, management is reviewing all of the deliverables at that particular phase-gate and determining whether the program has met the requirements to exit that particular phase and move onto the next.

Program reviews, on the other hand, are calendar based in that they occur at a regular interval independent of phase-gate status. These reviews provide a snapshot of the program's progress toward its objectives and alert senior management to issues and barriers to success.

Keys to Successful Program Reviews

The regular program review creates the organizational habit of regularly assessing the development program against its objectives. This not only serves as the regular update that senior management desires, but also forces the program manager to periodically evaluate the condition of the overall program. For program reviews to be effective, they need to:

1. Occur at least monthly to create an organizational habit.
2. Follow a consistent format anchored on program performance metrics so that the organization is able to easily evaluate the data being presented and identify changes, issues, and barriers.
3. Be regularly attended by senior management to reinforce the seriousness of accurate and complete program reporting and also to drive continuous improvement of the program review process.

Deciding who attends the program review is also important in determining the review's effectiveness. The review should not be an open forum where the whole organization gets a development program update. Doing this would fill the meeting with multiple levels of management and individual contributors, making it impossible for senior management to address tough issues or perhaps express dissatisfaction with program management.

To ensure open and frank discussions on tough issues that bubble up between program and senior management, always keep general audience program updates separate from formal program reviews. Program review attendees should include:

1. The senior management team members accountable for defining, developing, and delivering new products.
2. The program manager plus the few key members of the program's core team needed to ensure that senior management's questions will be answered.

What to Include in a Program Review

There are really only seven things that a business needs to know about its product development programs to determine whether or not they are on track. They are:

1. Status vs. top product lifecycle (PLC) milestones
2. Status vs. PLC deliverables
3. Status vs. success criteria
4. Status vs. product cost targets
5. Status vs. development cost targets

6. Top issues, risks, and action plan
7. Accomplishments/Goals for last/next month

Design your program reviews in a consistent format around these seven items, and you'll have a concise and precise status of your program and its key issues.

Status vs. Top PLC Milestones

It seems obvious that program milestones need to be tracked, but the trick is how they get tracked. Let's face it, executives look at a lot of different programs, so assessing whether a date is on target or not can be difficult.

First, the top level milestones should reflect the key milestones of your PLC process. This makes sure that the organization is using a consistent language for communicating new product development status. Second, track and report three dates for each milestone.

1. Baseline
2. Last report
3. This report

The baseline date is the original commitment set at the program start, and it never changes. The second is the date presented at the last review, and the third is the date presented at the current review.

By tracking these dates, you always have the answers to these two questions:

1. How have the milestone dates changed since the program was launched?
2. How have the milestone dates changed since the last review?

During a review, it's important to poke at the quality of the high-level milestone dates by periodically asking to see the detailed schedule. Also, alarms should go off when near-term milestones keep slipping but later dates are holding firm. When that happens, it's time to drill down by asking to see a recovery plan. See the figure 17 for an example template for tracking PLC milestones.

PLC Milestones	Baseline MM/DD/YY	Last Report MM/DD/YY	This Report MM/DD/YY
Phase I: Definition	**MM/YYYY**	**MM/YYYY**	**MM/YYYY**
■ MRD Approved	MM/YYYY	MM/YYYY	MM/YYYY
■ Product Plan Approved	MM/YYYY	MM/YYYY	MM/YYYY
Phase II: Design	**MM/YYYY**	**MM/YYYY**	**MM/YYYY**
■ Design Complete	MM/YYYY	MM/YYYY	MM/YYYY
■ Subsystem Verification	MM/YYYY	MM/YYYY	MM/YYYY
Phase III: System Verification	**MM/YYYY**	**MM/YYYY**	**MM/YYYY**
■ System Verification	MM/YYYY	MM/YYYY	MM/YYYY
■ Marathon Test	MM/YYYY	MM/YYYY	MM/YYYY
Phase IV: System Validation	**MM/YYYY**	**MM/YYYY**	**MM/YYYY**
■ Beta System Shipment	MM/YYYY	MM/YYYY	MM/YYYY
■ Specification Field Validated	MM/YYYY	MM/YYYY	MM/YYYY
Phase V: Production	**MM/YYYY**	**MM/YYYY**	**MM/YYYY**
■ Specification Set	MM/YYYY	MM/YYYY	MM/YYYY
■ Market Announcement	MM/YYYY	MM/YYYY	MM/YYYY

Figure 17: Sample Layout for Reporting PLC Milestones

Status vs. PLC Deliverables

A PLC process also describes the cross-functional deliverables for each phase of the process. It's important that these also be tracked and reported at a high level. This ensures that the program is being managed in the context of your PLC process and serves as a reminder to the program manager to constantly keep the "whole product" in view and not just the engineering.

Probably the easiest way to do this is to create a table of PLC deliverables by phase like the one in the figure 18, and then color code each cell in the table to indicate the status of each deliverable.

Status vs. Success Criteria

When the program was first defined, the product that it is supposed to produce had a set of performance objectives or success criteria. Select the most important ones and include them in each program review. These are usually the ten to fifteen most important buying

Phase 1 Definition	Phase 2 Design	Phase 3 Verification	Phase 4 Validation	Phase 5 Production
MRD	Design Spec.	Alpha Sys Build	Regulatory Sign-off	Selling Spec.
Product Plan	System Test Plan	Market Intro Plan	Production BOM	Market Intro Ready
Core Team	Sourcing Plan	System Test	Service Ready	Market Announcement
	Subsystem Test	Marathon Test	Operations Ready	Program Close Ready
	Product Design	Service Plan	1st System Shipped	
			Field Spec. Validation	

Figure 18: Sample PLC Cross-Functional Deliverables by Phase

criteria for the product that you're developing. For capital equipment products, it is also helpful to break these into two groups, one for process performance specifications and a second for cost of ownership specifications

Avoid any goals that aren't specific and measurable. There's a big difference between defining an objective as "improve throughput" versus "235 units per hour." The second objective will ensure that management and the program team have the same definition of success.

To track progress, create a table that lists the success criteria and target specifications. Then, create columns for each major level of testing that your PLC process outlines. For example, your PLC process may call for subsystem, full system, and field testing. See the example shown in figure 19. As the program progresses, enter the performance achieved into each cell of the table and color code each to indicate overall status. Develop color codes for:

1. Not yet tested
2. Test started—no results yet
3. Test complete—passed
4. Test complete—failed

Status vs. Product Cost Targets

At the end of the day, you'll want to have a full understanding of the cost of goods sold for your new product, the goal for which should have been spelled out at the program launch. This includes material, labor, warranty, installation, and overhead costs. However, during the early stages of a capital equipment development program, it will be difficult to collect solid data on anything except material costs.

Item	Specification	Phase 2 Sub-System Verification	Phase 3 System Verification	Phase 4 Field Validation
Process				
Process Spec Item 1	+/- 2.5%			
Process Spec Item 2	<1%			
Process Spec Item 3	<1%			
Process Spec Item 4	<1E19			
Process Spec Item 5	<25 @.12μm			
Cost of Ownership				
CoO Spec Item 1	>450 WPH			
CoO Spec Item 2	6 hrs			
CoO Spec Item 3	6			
CoO Spec Item 4	$120K/year			

Figure 19: Sample Template for Reporting Status vs. Success Criteria

That's not an issue, because material cost is the most important to understand. It is usually 60–80 percent of the total product cost and a key indicator for warranty-associated costs. Also, projections for labor, overhead, and installation costs don't become meaningful until the later phases of product development. Until then, they are just goals. This doesn't mean that the program shouldn't be taking action to hit these targets; it just means that measurements in early stages of product development aren't that valuable.

So, the approach for tracking costs in a program review is to develop detailed tracking for material costs, then lay out the data into a model that reflects your goal for total costs.

One way to track material cost is to use the product's family tree to create a cost status dashboard. Take the intended product structure summarized to somewhere between the first three to five levels. Format this like an organization chart so that it fits on one presentation slide. Each box represents a subsystem of the product.

In each box, document the material cost goal and the current projection. Top level boxes are summations of subordinate boxes.

To indicate the quality of the cost projections, color code each box to indicate how much of the subsystem has supplier commitment on costs. This can be done at four levels:

1. Engineering estimate only
2. Supplier commitment on 33 percent
3. Supplier commitment on 66 percent
4. Supplier commitment on 100 percent

This also serves the dual purpose of giving you a sense of how engaged supply chain management is in the process. At any rate, the top level of this diagram contains the current estimate of the material costs that can then be laid into the total cost profile for the product.

Status vs. Development Cost Targets

Annual development costs for a new capital equipment product can easily top ten million dollars, and that's why it's important to track program spending.

Develop a chart like the one in figure 20 to track periodic program spending versus budget. Watch for any departures from expected spending rates and demand that your program managers explain why it is different from the budget. Also, don't assume that under spending is a good sign; it could mean that your program is behind schedule.

Top Issues, Risks, and Action Plan

Have the program manager list the top three to five issues or risks to the program. These can be schedule, cost, or product performance risks. This step not only highlights the top issues, but it also forces program managers to sort through all of the noise and identify where they should be spending their time.

These top issues can be captured in a table like the one in figure 21.

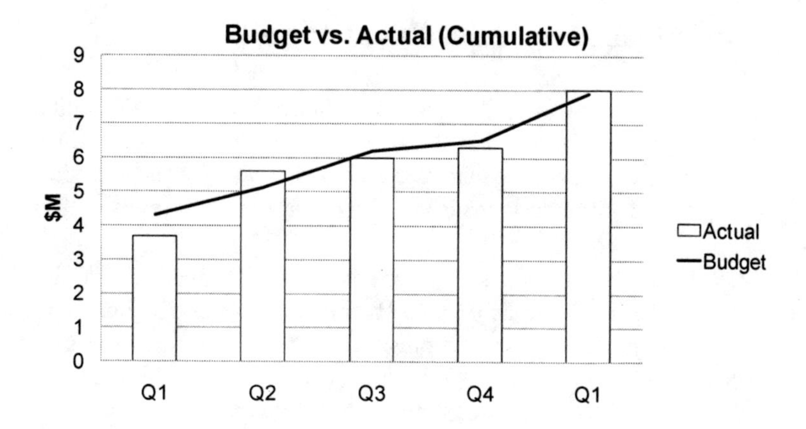

Figure 20: Sample Template for Tracking Program Status vs. Budget

Issue or Risk Problem Statement	Action Required	Who	When	Outlook

Figure 21: Sample Template for Tracking Development Program Top Issues

For each issue or risk, require an action plan. For the purposes of a senior management review, this plan should be concise and precise at the same time. For each issue, the program manager should indicate:

1. Issue or risk problem statement
2. Action steps
3. Owner(s)
4. Completion date
5. Outlook for success

Accomplishments Last/Next Month

This is the sanity check for whether the top-level milestones are supported by tangible progress and detailed action planning. Have the program manager list detailed accomplishments and goals for the two-month window surrounding your program review.

Each month, you should see last month's goals checked off as this month's accomplishments. If you don't, then it's likely that your top-level milestones are slipping. Also, make sure that next month's goals really cover what is needed to hit upcoming milestones. For example, if the thirty-day goal states: "Start ordering parts," and the top-level milestone says: "Ship next week," then there is a major disconnect.

4. The Roadmap Six-Pack

High-technology capital equipment can take years to develop. Even in a world in which that was all you had to worry about, long-term product planning would still be a considerable challenge. But it isn't all that you have to worry about. You also have to contend with a constantly changing technology, market, and competitive environment. If you have any hope of sustaining a competitive advantage over the long term, you're going to need a well-thought-out product roadmap to guide you.

Product roadmaps represent the steps that you will take to implement your strategy. They describe where you're headed and what products will be introduced along the way. Internally, they are used to guide the company and to synchronize the organization's efforts and investments. Externally, they can be used to attract customers, investors, and partners.

Many companies' product roadmaps, however, never get beyond simple graphical representations of product release timing. While these cursory roadmaps may help to communicate plans at a high level, they do very little to ensure alignment to a strategy that will meet market requirements and beat the competition.

For roadmaps to be an effective product management tool, they need to be more than just a short-hand snapshot of the company's current product development plans. To be effective, roadmaps should directly link to your:

1. Customers' roadmap
2. Competitors' strategy

This is difficult to do in a single superficial roadmap. A suite of six roadmaps is required, with each element creating a link in the chain that connects your product plans to what will win in the market. The six roadmaps and their contents are summarized in table 9.

Table 9: The Roadmap Six-pack and Its Contents

Roadmap Name	Contents
1. Industry	Technology changes and performance targets for your customers' products over time
2. Applications	Minimum requirements for your product to support the industry roadmap
3. Top-Level Product	Top-level product plan to address the applications roadmap and create competitive advantage
4. Requirements	Performance requirements for each product on the top-level roadmap in competitive context
5. Architecture	Top-level development and platform strategy to implement the requirements roadmap
6. External	A light version of the top-level product roadmap for external use

The roadmap six-pack is developed in that order, starting with an external perspective and progressing inward until it defines your plans for product implementation.

Industry Roadmap

The word "industry" in the industry roadmap refers to the industry that will buy your products. Think of it as your customers' product roadmap. It includes technology changes and performance targets over time for your customers' products.

Some industries publish a standard roadmap that can be used as a starting point for industry roadmap development like the semiconductor industry's International Roadmap for Semiconductors (I.T.R.S.).

In cases where an industry roadmap exists, it is usually developed by a consensus of an industry consortium's member companies. However, as an equipment supplier it would be a mistake to assume that this published industry roadmap is actually your customers' roadmap. It is not. It's a watered down, pre-competitive version of what industry consortium members are doing and thinking. It's like the external version of your own roadmap. The dates are padded, and a lot of the specifics are left out. While a published industry roadmap is a good place to start, it's not very useful for high-resolution product strategy development.

In the case of small or emerging industries without a consensus roadmap, it's often up to the supply chain (including equipment suppliers) selling into the industry to first aggregate an overall industry roadmap. The supply chain, in an effort to develop its own roadmaps, surveys the industry participants about their future plans and then synthesizes the results into an industry roadmap. Since the industry participants can't get past their competitors' lobbies, it's not surprising that the supply chain often has the best overall view of what's going on in the industry.

This is exactly how it happened when I was an equipment supplier to the manufacturers of high brightness light emitting diodes (HB-LEDs) in the early days of the industry. I needed to develop a product roadmap, but this young industry didn't have a roadmap of its own to guide me. It took many months of customer interviews before I had a multi-year roadmap drafted that described cost, brightness, efficiency, and reliability targets for HB-LEDs.

At the time, I simply viewed this accomplishment as a necessary first step to feed my roadmap six-pack. It wasn't until I presented my version of the industry roadmap to the CEO of a major HB-LED manufacturer in Taiwan that I realized how significant it was. Through the whole presentation, I didn't get a lot of feedback or reaction. However, at the end, the CEO asked me if he could have a copy of the presentation to show to his board of directors. He confessed that he had never developed or seen a roadmap for his own industry. The one that I had created as a supplier was the first one that he had ever laid eyes on.

Whether you participate in an industry that publishes a roadmap or not, you're going to have to roll up your sleeves to develop a roadmap with enough resolution to guide your product strategy. This means:

- Engaging with industry-leading companies and the people in those companies that are in charge of thinking about the future.
- Attending technology conferences for hints on what thoughts the leaders are experimenting with.
- Talking to your customers' customers to find out what they are demanding for future capability. Ask to see specification sheets for your customers' products, and then ask how they are likely to change in the future.
- Asking customers "why" when they ask you to participate in joint development ventures or experiments to gain an understanding of the request's context in the customer's overall long-term strategy.

Organize the results of this work into your own industry roadmap. Typically, this is done in tabular form like the fictitious roadmap example in figure 22, with technical attributes and performance metrics in the first column followed by columns for each year. These columns in your roadmap are filled in with targets and technology element descriptions. Just remember that you are creating your customers' roadmap and not yours in this step. So, it should be expressed in the terms of your customers' business, not yours.

Any Industry Roadmap					
	Year 1	Year 2	Year 3	Year 4	Year 5
Cost ($)	2.20	2.10	2.00	1.80	1.75
Lifetime (hrs)	2000	8000	15000	20000	25000
Defects (ppm)	100	80	75	60	40
Substrate Size (mm)	300	300	300	450	450
Die size (mm)	14	14	12	12	10
Device Architecture	Planar	Planar	Planar	3D	3D

Figure 22: Industry Roadmap Layout Example

The Applications Roadmap

The applications roadmap describes what you as a supplier must do at a minimum to meet the requirements of the industry roadmap. The two key things that you need to understand to create an applications roadmap are:

1. Industry roadmap
2. Implications for your product

The implications for your product are the changes that the industry roadmap will impose on the purchasing specifications for your product. For example, if the industry roadmap describes targets for improving production yields, the implication for your product may be to reduce defects in the manufacturing step that your product performs.

Constructing the applications roadmap from this point is pretty straightforward. In form, it is similar to the industry roadmap. First, list the most important application requirements. These are usually key purchasing criteria for your product. Then describe how each of these will change over time in response to the industry roadmap. See figure 23 for an example.

Any Thin-Film Application Roadmap					
	Year 1	Year 2	Year 3	Year 4	Year 5
Film Chemistry	C, In, Se	C, In, Se, Ga	C, In, Se, Ga	C, In, Se, Ga	C, In, Se, Ga, Na
Min. Film Thickness	.4μm	.4μm	.3μm	.3μm	.2μm
Film Non-Uniformity	1.0%	1.0%	1.0%	1.0%	1.0%
Process Temperature	600°C	600°C	600°C	450°C	450°C
Substrate Material	Glass	Glass	Glass	Glass Polyimide	Glass Polyimide
Max. Substrate Width	30cm	30cm	1M	1M	1M

Figure 23: Applications Roadmap Example

For high-tech capital equipment, the applications roadmap is usually populated with process requirements rather than cost of ownership requirements. Generally, cost of ownership targets are set by the competitive landscape rather than by an industry application requirement. These targets are usually developed in roadmaps three and four of the roadmap six-pack.

It's also important to note that the applications roadmap does not describe the performance targets necessary for you to win business; it only describes the targets you must meet in order to be considered. Winning business requires both meeting applications requirements and doing it better than the competition. How to do that is coming up in the next two roadmaps.

Top-Level Product Roadmap

With the industry and applications roadmap finished, you're ready to create the first representation of your plan to develop and introduce products with your top-level product roadmap. This roadmap will be a very high-level description of:

1. Product introduction timing

2. Important performance targets
3. Top-level product architecture

This roadmap takes the familiar form of a graphical representation of new product release timing. However, the most important aspect of this roadmap is that you will not only lay out the above for your product, but you will also do the same for your competitors' products. The result is a top-level view of your product strategy in the context of your competitive environment. See figure 24 for an example.

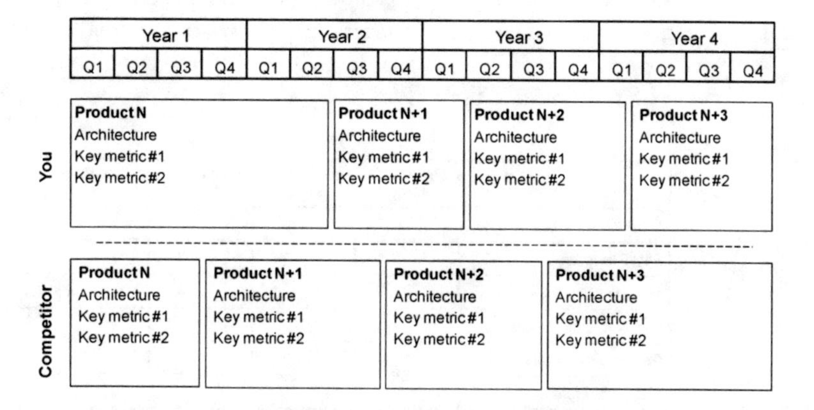

Figure 24: Sample Top-Level Roadmap

This step in roadmap development is very helpful to analyze and communicate how the competitive environment evolves over the timeframe that your roadmap covers. At a glance, you can see how you compare to the competition on product release timing, architecture selection, and key metric performance. The most difficult portion of the roadmap to accurately develop is your competitors' strategy. However, unless you know it, you won't be able to evaluate the likelihood of your strategy succeeding.

Since roadmaps are a carefully guarded secret, you'll never know your competitors' plans with complete certainty. However, you need to assemble all of the clues gathered from customers, sales and service people, conferences, and suppliers to get your best understanding of their strategy. You may surprise yourself with just how much information you can assemble by deciding to focus on it.

The Requirements Roadmap

With the requirements roadmap, the description of each product represented on the top-level roadmap needs to be expanded to include a broader set of performance requirements. Again, this will be done in the context of the competition.

To create this roadmap, you'll select the application and cost of ownership performance metrics most important to the purchasing decision for products like yours, and then specify the performance targets for each of the products in your roadmap. You'll also include your competitors' current and expected future capability on the same set of metrics. See figure 25.

	Product N Now	Product N+1 Date	Product N+2 Date	Comp. N Now	Comp. N+2 Date
Process					
Film Chemistry					
Min. Film Thickness					
Film Non-Uniformity					
Process Temperature					
Substrate Material					
Cost of Ownership					
Throughput					
Setup time					
Uptime (%)					
System Material Cost					
Annual Consumables Cost					

Figure 25: Sample Requirements Roadmap

In the sample layout above, each empty cell in the table is populated with the performance target for each product. The last two columns are for your competitors' current performance and performance at the end of the roadmap period. This allows a quick evaluation of how you are likely to compete over time if you meet your performance targets. To make the comparison even more obvious, color code each cell containing performance targets for your products. For example, where you have advantage, color code the cell "green"; where you are neutral, try "yellow"; and where you have a disadvantage, color the cell "red."

Creating the performance requirements roadmap this way will also start to reveal your competitive strategy. Your vision for competitive advantage shows up as the critical few performance metrics you are driving to be substantially better than the competition. Equally important are those metrics that you are prescribing to only meet the competitive threshold.

The Architecture Roadmap

The requirements roadmap enables the organization to plan its product architecture strategy. The architecture roadmap is the top-level description of that strategy. It will describe platforms and subsystems to be used, reused, and/or newly designed.

The architecture roadmap looks a lot like the performance roadmap, but instead of performance metrics and targets, it contains subsystems and subsystem architecture descriptions. See figure 26.

	Product N Now	**Product N+1 Date**	**Product N+2 Date**
Subsystem 1			
Subsystem 2			
Subsystem 3			
Subsystem 4			
Subsystem 5			
Subsystem 6			
Subsystem N			

Figure 26: Sample Architecture Roadmap Layout

In the architecture layout sample, the left column contains the general description of each of the major subsystems of your product. For example, if you manufacture thin film deposition process equipment, you might have subsystems such as:

1. Process chambers
2. Deposition source
3. Control system
4. Substrate handler
5. Facilities module

It's also good practice to use one of the subsystem rows for "Platform Name" so that your architecture roadmap is explicit about the product platform that will be used for each product generation.

Then, for each subsystem, enter a shorthand name or description for the platform or design architecture to be used for each of the products in the roadmap.

Finally, indicate whether subsystems in each product are:

1. Reused from previous designs
2. Modified versions of previous designs
3. New designs

Again, use a green, yellow, red color code for each of the three subsystem categories, respectively, to quickly communicate the amount of subsystem redesign in each product generation. This last step helps to communicate the design risk plus the time and money needed for development. For example, a lot of red (new designs) on the architecture roadmap typically indicates that more money and time is needed than one with mostly green (reuse) and yellow (modified previous designs).

The product requirements and product architecture roadmaps should align. At the most basic level, the number of products and planned introduction dates should align. But also, changes in performance requirements should reconcile with the changes in the architecture roadmap.

The External Roadmap

This is easy if you have completed the first five roadmaps in the six-pack. This is simply a light version of the top-level product roadmap. To create it, take your top-level roadmap and:

1. Remove references to the competition.
2. Remove references to system architecture.
3. Make references to performance metrics directional instead of absolute. For example instead of "500 units/hour" put "improved throughput."
4. Shift introduction dates to the right.
5. Extend life of all products to cover the full duration of the roadmap to avoid pre-announcing any product's end-of-life.

When you are done, it will look like the sample in figure 27.

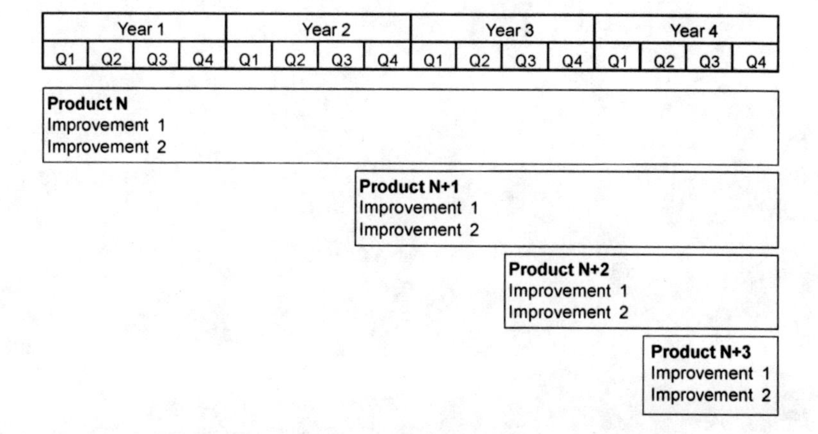

Figure 27: Sample External Product Roadmap Layout

Whenever sharing an external roadmap, make sure to always tag it with the caveat that it represents your company's current plans, which are subject to change, and that it does not represent specific customer commitments.

5. Why No One Reads Your Market Requirements Document

The Market Requirements Document or MRD is probably the most important strategy tool in the capital equipment product manager's toolbox. However, how best to use it is not always understood, and the tool itself is not always put together very well. As a result, MRDs get written, but they don't always get read.

It's not uncommon for an organization to be confused about what they're supposed to do with an MRD once it's developed. Sometimes it's just dismissed as some irrelevant document produced by the marketing department. Take notice if you've heard comments like these:

- "I don't know why we need an MRD. What really matters is the engineering development plan."
- "Just give me the product specs. I don't care about all that marketing fluff."
- "Why do I have to sign this?"

- "We should just combine the MRD and the engineering development plan documents to save time."

Comments like these could mean that your organization is missing the whole point of an MRD. Success doesn't just come from building the product right; it also requires that you build the right product. It's the MRD that guides the organization to make robust decisions about which products to select. For the MRD to do its job, however, the organization needs to understand where it fits in the product decision-making process, and MRD authors need to structure it to support this decision making.

What an MRD Is and What It Is Not

An MRD is a business case for investing in an opportunity and a description of the product requirements that will satisfy that business case. It defines for whom the product exists, what it must do, and how well it must perform in order to capture customers and make a profit.

An MRD is not a product development plan nor does it necessarily represent what an organization is capable of doing. It is very important to keep MRD's and Product Development Plans (PDP's) separate. By keeping these separate, you can always evaluate whether or not a PDP will satisfy the business case for the product by comparing it to the MRD. If you don't, you run the risk of blurring the line between "what needs to be done" and "what the organization knows how to do." As a result, you can end up making product investment decisions based on internal capability and not on what customers will actually buy. You could end up building the product right, but not necessarily building the right product.

Also, an MRD does not change as a result of changes in the PDP. The "MR" in MRD is for "Market Requirements," and market requirements don't change just because a supplier cannot meet them. The MRD changes if the market changes and, in turn, that may require changes to the PDP—but not the other way around.

Also the PDP and MRD do not have to be perfectly aligned to have a sound product plan. A PDP may not address every product requirement exactly as specified in the MRD. This isn't an automatic show stopper. It's possible that if the PDP satisfies enough of the business case, or satisfies it differently than the MRD described, it may still be a worthy endeavor.

Table 10: Differences between an MRD and a PDP

MRD	PDP
Business case and product requirements	Development schedule, resources, budget, and product performance targets
What needs to be done	What can be done

Evaluating and Approving an MRD

MRD approval should be a major and formal phase gate in any product lifecycle management process. It's where you decide whether or not a product should be developed. How to make this decision can be difficult for some organizations, since management usually spends most of its time trying to figure out how to make products, not whether or not they should be making them.

To make decisions on whether or not a product is worth pursuing, seek the answers to these questions when reviewing an MRD.

For the business case, ask:

- Is the opportunity real?
- Is it worth pursuing?
- Can we win?

For the product requirements, ask:

- If the product were introduced as described, would it satisfy the business case?

- Are product requirements clear enough to develop a PDP?

In evaluating the business case, be sure that there is clear evidence that a real problem exists in a market and that there are enough customers willing to pay for a solution. Winning is a function of your ability to conceive a unique, defendable, value proposition. It's worth it if forecasted returns are greater than the cost to capitalize on the opportunity; it also needs to fit with your company's overall strategy.

For the product requirements portion of the MRD, your focus is on the match between the product requirements and the business case as well as the clarity with which the requirements are described.

As a formal step in the product lifecycle process, the MRD will be formally approved or rejected depending on the MRD's ability to answer the previous questions. This approval does not launch a development program; it only launches the development of the PDP against a valid opportunity. Also, approving the MRD does not commit the organization to achieving the milestones and product performance that it describes. Only the PDP can do that.

Table 11: Differences between MRD and PDP Approvals

MRD Approval	PDP Approval
OK to proceed with PDP	OK to launch and fund program
Opportunity is valid	Plan substantially satisfies business case
Recommendation	Commitment

Write the MRD to Support Decision Making

The MRD must be written to provide the answers to the questions outlined in the previous section. This means that you have to go beyond just summarizing general market conditions and describing a product by setting all of the performance specifications to be better than your nearest competitor.

Table 12: MRD Business Case Section Outline

Business Case Section	Key Questions Answered
Objectives	• What are market share targets? • What are your gross margin targets? • When will they be achieved?
Market Forecast	• What is the total available market past, present, future? • How is the market segmented past, present, future? • What is the market growth rate and what is driving it?
Market Position	• What is your market share past and present? • What are your competitors' market shares past and present? • What will account for changes in market share?
Competition	• Who are the competitors? • What are their product offerings and strategy? • How does their product strategy compare to yours?
Target Customers/ Market	• Which customers or market segments will be pursued? • Which ones will not? • How do these customers add up to meet your objectives?
Vision for Competitive Advantage	• How will you win? • What is it about your company or current products that enable this vision? • How does your competitive advantage translate into a value proposition?
Potential Returns	• What is the incremental projected revenue and profit if the opportunity is successfully pursued? • What assumptions were made in your analysis?

The first step is to build the business case for the product that you're recommending. To do this, you need to develop a logical framework that outlines how pursuing this opportunity will help the company meet its objectives. One such outline is shown in table 12.

The product requirements' section should contain all of the elements of a new product that are required to realize the business case that you've laid out. This is much more than just a list of specifications. It also needs to describe the platform, installed base upgrades, availability, and testing requirements. See table 13.

Table 13: MRD Product Requirements Section Outline

Product Requirements Section	**Key Questions Answered**
Platform Requirements	• Which product platform(s) must be used? • Which common parts and interfaces with other products must be used?
Installed Base Upgrade Requirements	• What elements of the new product must be made available to the previous generation installed base? • What are the performance and cost targets?
Availability Requirements	• When is the product required in the market to hit the business case objectives? • What interim milestones must be hit to support marketing activity?
Performance Validation Requirements	• How does the new product need to be tested for it to reflect usage in the customers' environment?
Product Specifications	• Which performance and cost specifications must exceed competitive benchmarks in order to achieve vision for competitive advantage? • What are the performance and cost targets for everything else?

All of these requirements need to link back to the business case. The best test for whether you've got the product requirements right is to be able to satisfactorily answer the following questions for each item.

1. Why do you need it?
2. How do you know?

The measure of success for an MRD is not necessarily whether or not it gets approved; it's how well you've connected the dots to ensure that an organization can make informed, high-quality decisions about the opportunity and the product.

MRD at Work Case Study

A Tekcess International client had been developing a new piece of processing equipment for the semiconductor industry. The technology was novel and had generated a lot of "tire kicking" from prospects. However, after more than two years of product development and dozens of customer demonstrations, not a single dollar of revenue had been generated.

The management team was split on what to do with this product. Its advocates felt that a breakthrough was just around the corner, and its detractors were tired of investing without a return. Internal debates, although passionate on both sides, weren't going anywhere because they didn't have a solid framework for making the right decision.

To resolve the dilemma, we navigated the organization through a solid MRD process. The idea of going back and developing an MRD for an existing product development program may seem strange, but in this case it was necessary in order to reach a consensus decision on the fate of this program.

We revisited the entire business case, which revealed that the market opportunity was much smaller than originally thought. Additionally, the product that was needed to capture any meaningful value would require substantially more time and money in order to bring it to market.

At the end of the process, it was decided that the program should be cancelled. Once the organization worked through a logical framework for selecting products, it became clear that a business case for continuing this product did not exist. At first, the product manager felt like he had failed the organization. However, the opposite was true. He had just saved the company millions of dollars a year that could now be allocated to high-return programs.

6. Market Requirements Are Not Negotiable

It took one of those heavy duty staplers to secure the pages of your Market Requirements Document (MRD). You're a seasoned professional, so knew to ask for more product capability than you really need. That way you'll emerge from your negotiation with engineering with a plan that you can live with.

But engineering knows how you work. They've padded the schedule and held back on performance commitments.

Let the bargaining begin.

In many organizations, this is how the game is played. In fact, a capital equipment CEO once said to me, "Marketing asks for 100 percent; engineering commits to 80 percent of the marketing request and then delivers 80 percent of their commitment. That's just how it works, so you have to write your MRD accordingly."

But, the idea that somehow you can negotiate market requirements is fundamentally flawed. Market requirements are independent of what an individual supplier can do. They are 100 percent about what your customers need in order to be successful in their own businesses.

This negotiation mindset leads to product managers bloating their MRDs to overshoot what they really need and, as a result, you never wind up with a document that actually describes the true market requirements. Therefore, the piecemeal negotiation with engineering is almost guaranteed to result in a product definition that's far from the coherent whole that the market really needs.

There's a better way. It requires that product management define lean, whole products and that they take the necessary steps to avoid big disconnects with engineering.

Lean Definition of a Whole Product

First, product management needs to turn its mindset inside out. Instead of asking for more than it needs as a hedge, it needs to seek a product definition that will achieve business objectives with the least amount of engineering effort. It might go against your instincts, but the MRD must describe what is needed to satisfy the business case for a product and nothing more.

To accomplish this, follow this four-step process.

1. Select a market segment big enough to support your objectives with plenty of customers who have similar buying behaviors and product needs.
2. Define the vision for competitive advantage including the value proposition and the supporting product positioning.
3. Set performance levels to exceed those of your competitors for product attributes that make up your competitive advantage.
4. Set requirements on all other performance attributes to only meet, not beat, the market need.

Notice that you are not going to set all product performance attributes to be better than those of the competition. This is not necessary and is a waste of engineering time and money. You're looking to be the best at the few things that really fulfill the vision for competitive advantage and drive customers' purchasing decisions. For everything else, you're going to target being "just good enough."

An automotive industry example can help illustrate this point. Volvo, a Swedish car manufacturer, creates competitive advantage by producing the safest cars. Compared to their competitors, their cars have the most complete and most technically advanced safety features. However, their gas mileage, engine power, and interior appointments are "just good enough," not exceptional. This is their version of a lean product.

By only stretching the organization on key competitive drivers, you will reduce the time, cost, and risk in your product development program. Your result should be a product definition that addresses market requirements to a degree that will hit the business objectives without extras tossed in.

To ensure that you've set targets that will both meet customer requirements and win their business, you'll need to test your MRD with key customers. This should be a formal process in which you will validate:

1. Product performance targets
2. Release timing
3. Value proposition and product positioning

This critical step ensures that you've covered all of your bases and defined a complete product for your target market. As a result, you'll have a lean definition of a whole product. That definition is lean because you set out with a "least engineering, most result" mindset. You know that it's whole because you've tested it with your target market. Because it's both lean and whole, it represents true market needs that are not negotiable.

How to Avoid Big Disconnects with Engineering

The "market requirements are non-negotiable" position is not designed to set up a confrontation with engineering, establish an ultimatum position, or imply that an MRD can just be thrown over the wall to engineering. You still have to find the intersection of those needs and your ability to develop products to meet them. This will require creativity, an open mind, and a healthy working relationship with the development team.

It's a recipe for failure to exclude engineering when developing market requirements. Failure to maintain open, active lines of communication between product management and engineering can lead to big disconnects between what the market needs and what the organization is capable of delivering. This, in turn, leads to late deliveries and products that fail to meet business objectives.

Applying these three simple practices will help your product management and product development teams work together to avoid major disconnects.

1. Educate each other
2. Use the "What, Why, How" principle
3. Bring in outside forces

Product management should take the lead and conduct regular forums with engineering on emerging market trends, customer challenges, and the competitive environment. Likewise, engineering should educate product management on available technologies, new ways to use existing technologies, product development issues, and technical trade-offs. The more product management and engineering understand each other, the more likely they are to produce winning products.

The "What, Why, and How" principle is very helpful when things get heated in the give and take between product management and engineering. When there is an issue on the table that product management and engineering cannot agree on, the first thing to do is figure out where the issue fits in the "What, Why, and How" construct. To apply this principle, first get agreement on which of the following best describes the issue that is being debated:

- What is needed?
- Why it is needed?
- How the need is to be addressed?

Many times, it can appear that engineering is challenging a market requirement, but when examined through the "What, Why, How" lens, you may find that it's not the requirement (what) that is being questioned but rather the approach (how). By the same token, it's also common for product management to passionately defend what appears to be a market requirement when, under closer examination, it turns out that the market requirement (a what) was really a solution (a how).

In general, product management should be the steward of "what" and be able to defend it with "why." Engineering's primary concern is to understand the "what" and "why" well enough to figure out the "how."

Finally, one of the best ways to cultivate buy-in for market requirements is to bring in external forces. Don't insulate engineering from direct contact with your market. Expose them to customers by taking them on requirements gathering missions, and even let them observe the battle over a particularly competitive purchase order. This direct contact with the real market will help engineering to internalize what the market really needs better than even the most eloquently written MRD could do.

For a product to be successful, the engineering team must be motivated to address the market requirements. The more they understand the context of market problems, the more creative and relevant their proposed solutions will be.

Good product management is more than producing a lean definition of a whole product to address market needs. It's also the ability to develop the understanding across the organization so that the market needs can be connected to a winning solution.

7. You Built It, but Will They Buy It?

Your new product meets specifications. It was released on time, and it came in under budget.

That's all good news, but will anyone buy it.

A well-run development program isn't enough to ensure a market winner. You have to commit yourself every step of the way to uncover, in exquisite detail, exactly what the market needs and how it will react to your new product.

The products that customers buy are those that solve their problems the best, whether those are your products or the products of the competition. That means you'll need to score a bulls eye on:

1. Technology and timing
2. Performance targets
3. Product design
4. Design implementation

Hitting the center of the dartboard at product launch depends on how well you validated your product with target customers on all four elements.

Market validation for capital equipment products can be thought of as two distinct processes. One is roadmap validation and the other is new product validation. Roadmap validation is where you frame your company's roadmap for new product timing and technology in terms of market needs. This is an iterative process. The conclusions reached about the market needs and timing trigger new product development programs.

Then each of these new product development programs must include a much more detailed market validation process to ensure that it has set the right targets, has addressed them with the right design, and has produced the right implementation of that design. The framework for market validation is summarized in figure 28.

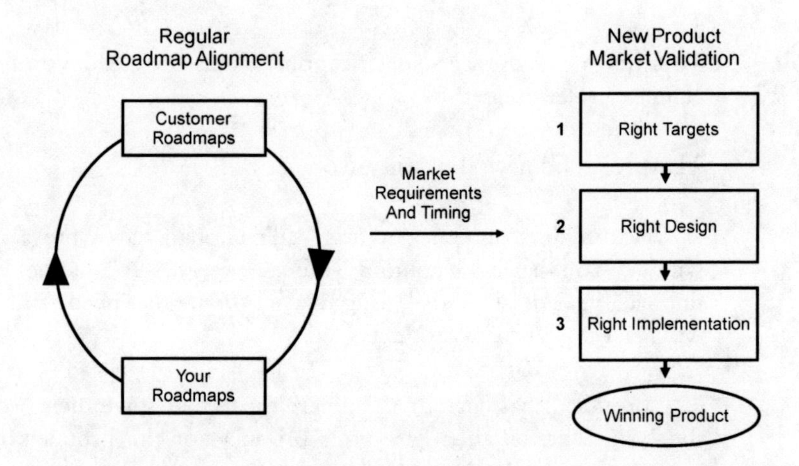

Figure 28: Framework for Capital Equipment Market Validation

Technology and Timing

Sharing roadmaps is a customer expectation in most high-technology capital equipment industries. Customers want suppliers to share their plans for the future so that they can:

- Be sure that you'll be able to meet their requirements.
- Be aware of potential savings or profit-generating opportunities.
- Understand their technical options for addressing their issues.

Sharing your roadmap also helps you to build credibility and improve your relationships by demonstrating a real understanding of your customers' business. It's a form of market research that elicits customer reactions to generate practical information in order to validate market needs plus your company's strategy and product plans.

What you're looking for in this phase of market validation are your customers' technology requirements and when those technologies will be required. With this information, you can determine when new products are needed as well as the general technical and performance specifications. To get the most out of your roadmap validation process:

- Share your view of the industry's challenges. Describe what you understand the requirements to be as well as how and when you plan to address them. Your customers will be more open about their plans if you share yours.
- Resist the urge to "sell" or get defensive about your roadmap and strategy. If the customer objects to a roadmap item, seek first to understand the concern and spend less time trying to defend your position. Remember that you're not selling anything other than the fact that you are a first-rate supplier that seeks to understand customer needs.
- Focus on the industry, applications, and external roadmaps from your roadmap six-pack. You should be more concerned with what is needed and why it's needed than with your specific product implementation plans at this point.
- Don't tie roadmap validation frequency or timing to product plans. This is a continuous process, so make it a regular habit. At a minimum, try to get in front of each key customer at least once or twice a year.
- Let customers know well in advance of a roadmap visit that you will be sharing your roadmap and would like for them to share

theirs. Alert them to any specific areas that you'll be probing. This gives them time to prepare and makes the best use of your time.

- Talk 20 percent and listen 80 percent of the time in roadmap-sharing meetings; one-half of your talking time should be devoted to asking meaningful questions.

This process will create a steady stream of input. Constantly evaluate and reconcile this data to identify technology and timing requirements for your company's new products.

Right Performance Targets

Your validated roadmap will now spawn the need to develop a Market Requirements Document (MRD) to make a business case and outline performance targets for a new product.

To ensure that you've set targets that will meet customer requirements and win their business, test them long before you begin cutting metal. In this step, get specific about requirements and timing. Think of this as high-resolution roadmap validation.

To test the "win their business" part, you need to identify your vision for competitive advantage. This includes both your value proposition and the market positions that you will take.

Let's say your vision for competitive advantage included:

"To achieve the highest yields by producing the most uniform films with the lowest contamination levels …"

Make sure that yield, uniformity, and contamination performance make it to the top of your customers' selection criteria list. In this step, you are essentially asking, "If I built a product that did these things at this time, would you buy from me?"

To prepare for the MRD validation step, you'll need to prepare the following items:

- MRD

- List of customers in your target market
- Results from the MRD review with engineering to identify potential design trade-offs
- List of critical questions

From that point, you can assemble a "Performance Targets" validation toolkit to use with your customers that contains:

- Customer version of the MRD
- Critical questions questionnaire
- Attribute weighting exercise

The final item in the toolkit, the attribute weighting exercise, is a critical step in MRD validation. You'll need a tool for measuring how your customers rank performance attributes. For example, you need a way to get the answers to questions like these:

- Is process more important than productivity?
- Is productivity more important than defect control?
- Is defect control more important than price?

Several analytical tools are available that can help you to take customers through an exercise to generate this weighted ranking. This will give you insight about how your customers make trade-off decisions, which you can then use to guide trade-off decision making in your product design.

The critical questions questionnaire is just a collection of the important questions that must be answered to ensure that your MRD will put you on a winning path. Creating this questionnaire should be a formal process that involves the key stakeholders on the product team. The nature of the questions should focus on:

- Information needed to help make design trade-off decisions
- Details about performance requirements
- Information about the competition

- More resolution on the application
- Clarity on timing requirements

One thing that you are guaranteed to face is conflicting data. Your customers are not of one mind, nor do they all use and evaluate products the same way.

What's important is for you to understand what is driving the inconsistencies and how they will affect your vision for the product. To improve your ability to do that, use the same questionnaire, presentation materials, and validation team at every customer meeting. This eliminates many of the variables.

Right Product Design

Once the MRD is validated and signed off, and engineering is figuring out how to address the requirements, it's time to make sure that their interpretation of how to meet requirements will be embraced by your customers.

As soon as concept drawings and animations are available, showcase them to a subset of the same customers who saw your MRD. Also, don't forget to review the alternatives and performance trade-offs that your team is considering. Customer reaction to these can also be revealing.

You're looking for what customers like and don't like about your concept, and why. Again, stay away from "selling" or trying to defend your design. If you can force yourself to listen, you just might gain that pearl of insight that makes your product a winner.

After completing this step, decide what design changes make sense to improve market acceptance, and implement them.

Right Design Implementation

Of course, what really matters is product performance in the customers' environment. In this step, ship a pre-production or beta system to select customers for evaluation and feedback before full production shipments begin. This is a time and cash consuming step, so keep the number of customer engagements small.

For each beta-site evaluation, establish a formal agreement for:

- Qualification testing
- Data sharing
- Design changes
- Success criteria
- Terms for purchase

As with all steps, incorporate beta-site feedback into your design as appropriate.

It's no secret that this important step is often squeezed out of development programs that are running late. The secret to keeping it in place is to start your development program on time.

How to Talk to Customers about Future Products

In all of these validation steps, you will be talking to your customers and likely your sales force about products that are not yet for sale. This is a tricky situation that, if mishandled, can:

- Delay sales of your current products
- Tip your hand to competitors
- Over-commit your company

To manage expectations with sales and customers during the market validation process:

- Make sure that everyone involved understands that roadmaps and MRDs represent intentions, not commitments.
- Know where you are in the buying cycle with each customer and adjust your market validation process so that you don't discourage a customer from buying a current product.

- Require sales to repeat the following mantra at least three times: "Our current product is for sale, not the one on the roadmap or in the MRD."
- Keep market validation customer visits separate from sales calls.
- Never include any product cost information in market validation materials or discussions.
- Include a 3–6 month buffer on all future product release dates.

Whenever you are talking about future products, you are sharing the essence of your strategy, and there is always the risk that it will be leaked to competitors. It's always a balancing act to share enough to get meaningful feedback, and at the same time keep the information from the competition. To minimize that risk:

- Assume that information will be leaked to competitors. Review all materials to make sure that you're hitting the right balance between sharing and protecting information.
- Make sure that non-disclosure agreements are in place.
- Present and share, but never distribute market validation materials outside of your company.

Finally, in each market validation step, you are trying to obtain accurate information that will help you produce a product that customers will buy, at your price, over those of your competition. This means that you'll need to create an environment for each customer meeting that is conducive to free-flowing information. Some things to consider are:

- Small groups often work best. The bigger the meeting, the more formal it gets. The more formal it gets, the less information gets shared.
- Don't bring senior management to working-level meetings. This often stifles the information flow. If your customer knows that you are bringing your VP, then he will invite his. All of the sudden your relaxed exchange of information becomes a formal meeting between executives.
- Make sure that you have information to give as well as get.

- Get multiple perspectives within any given customer; for example, R&D, production, and management.
- The best size for the validation team is often two, plus a host from the account team. The two are usually a combination of a product management representative and a technical expert.
- Decide who is going to present materials and who is going to make sure that all of the critical questions get asked and answered.
- Before each meeting, select an appropriate questioning and presentation approach to match the customer's style, culture, meeting environment, and attendees.
- Keep the same team for each validation step to get a true handle on any conflicting customer feedback. Multiple teams will have multiple perceptions, which are difficult to manage.

8. Framework for a Successful Product Launch

Does your company tend to focus all of its product launch energy on the product announcement and first trade show, and then wonder why, a year later, sales objectives were missed and early customers are now unhappy?

You can blame it all on not recognizing that a successful product launch is a process and not just an event.

In capital equipment the product launch or market introduction process is a formal part of a new product program owned by the marketing representative on the product development team. This process must address all of the steps necessary to define the product, price it, produce it, promote it, and equip the sales team to sell it. It's a big task that requires formal planning, documentation, and communication.

Start the Process Early

The work on a product launch plan begins the moment the product development plan is approved. This plan is all that you need to begin thinking about how to launch the product.

You might ask, "How can I possibly start planning to market the product when the design hasn't even started?" The product development plan, if done correctly, describes the timing, specifications, costs, and design approach. From a market perspective, a product is just a set of specifications made available in a specific timeframe. How you get it to meet those specifications is largely irrelevant to product launch planning.

Since the product development plan has nearly everything that you need, you can get started planning your market introduction by simply assuming that the team will hit its goals. Of course, you are going to have to make revisions along the way, but it's a lot easier to make adjustments to a plan than it is to create one in the frenzied final innings of a product development program.

More importantly, the simple act of creating this draft and sharing it with the product team regularly will serve as an alignment mechanism. Before the program was launched, the market requirements document (MRD) served as this outside-in perspective of what the product needs to be in order to win in the market. But a year into the development program, it's easy to forget the contents of the MRD. Once the program is launched, you can use the market introduction plan to keep the organization focused on what it takes to acquire and keep customers.

Anatomy of the Product Launch Plan

Any product launch plan needs to answer five questions:

1. What are you going to sell?
2. Who are you going to sell it to?
3. Why will they buy?
4. How will you create demand?
5. When do key launch milestones occur?

It's just five questions, but a lot of detail, planning, and coordination is required to answer them. Table 14 outlines the details for each of the five questions.

Table 14: Key Questions for a Market Introduction Plan

Questions	Details
What are you going to sell?	• What is the name of the new product? • Does it replace an existing product? • What are the product specifications? • What upgrades are included for the installed base? • What is the product configuration(s)? • What are the product, options, and upgrades prices?
Who are you going to sell to?	• What is your target market? • Who are the key players in that market? • What is your plan to capture those key accounts? • Who will be your beta partner?
Why will they buy?	• What is the value metric that drives buying decisions? • What is your value proposition? • What makes your value unique? • How do your advantages influence buying decisions? • What data is needed to support your positions? • How do you compare to the competition? • How will the competition respond to your positioning?
How will you create demand?	• What is the product demonstration plan? • What sales presentations need to be developed? • What sales collateral will be created? • How and when will you train the sales force? • What are your press, events, and advertising plans? • What is the post announcement marketing plan?
When do key launch milestones occur?	• When will the product specifications be set? • When will the demonstration system be ready? • When will the sales kit be finished? • When will press and advertising materials be complete? • When will sales training be complete? • When will the beta system ship? • When will the first production system ship? • When will you announce the product?

Each of these components is critical to a successful product launch. It's a lot of work, and that is why it's always best to start launch planning early in the product development program.

What Can Go Wrong and What to Do

Capital equipment companies invest millions of dollars developing new products to improve profitability and market position. However, even when the development program has been executed flawlessly, it can all fall apart at product launch.

New product launches are high risk events that can hurt profitability, market position, and reputation when things go wrong. Here are five of the most common product launch failures and what to do to avoid them.

1. Money left on the table

   Pricing a product wrong or "over configuring" it will erode profit margins. Make sure that pricing is based on value, and keep base configurations to the minimum market expectation. Price extended capabilities and features separately.

   Make sure that you've equipped your sales force to articulate your value proposition, and make sure that they buy into it. A vigorous, well articulated, value-based, pricing defense will make them much better negotiators.

2. High support costs/Unhappy early adopters

   When a product goes to market and doesn't perform as expected right out of the box, two bad things happen; your support costs skyrocket and your early customers come down with a case of buyers' remorse. This combination can really stall a product launch.

   Two failures in product introduction execution create this situation. The first is failing to adequately test the new product in the same manner as your customer will use it. As a result, all of those early product defects that you should have found in your factory are discovered at your customers' site where they cost you more to fix in addition to disrupting your customers' business.

The second is setting selling specifications beyond the product's capability. Consequently, warranty costs will soar while the whole organization scrambles to fix broken promises.

Don't skimp on the testing phase of your development program. When the testing is complete, take the time to formally review test results vs. target specifications before you start making customer commitments.

3. Revenue chasm

When your customers stop buying your existing product in anticipation of the new product too early, you get a revenue chasm. To avoid this, carefully select the customers who are allowed a pre-announcement look at your new product.

In addition, it's essential to create a plan with the sales team, detailing how each customer will be transitioned to the new product.

Finally, during "voice of the customer exercises" leading up to the product launch, be vague enough about your new product plans to give yourself a cushion on release timelines.

4. Obsolete inventory

Nobody wants a warehouse full of parts for the old product, but if you fail to plan for the product transition, that is exactly what will happen. Early in your launch planning, create a production plan that forecasts the new and old product shipment mix for the six months before and the twelve months after the launch date.

5. Nobody wants to be first

In the case of capital equipment, customers are often wary of buying new systems before they've been vetted by somebody else.

To avoid this, ensure that product validation testing was conducted in as close to the real-world customer environment as possible, and include the data in your selling materials.

Also, don't let "beta" be just a code name for early production systems that aren't quite ready. Use a formal beta process to rapidly mature the system with a handful of key customers. Get testimonials from these early adopters to help you calm nervous prospects.

Finally, keep in pristine condition a demonstration system that is maintained and operated by a well-trained staff. Nothing kills the customer's view of a new system's maturity faster than a failed demo.

When you take the steps necessary to avoid these five product launch failures, you'll be on your way to a smooth production ramp, a better prepared sales force, happier customers, and a faster time-to-profit.

9. Six Ways to Improve Pricing

Think quickly! What would you do to improve gross margins at your company?

Did you think, "Reduce costs?" Most people do.

But what if you could raise prices? Wouldn't that be the fastest way to improve margins? You'd expect price improvement programs to be as common as cost reduction efforts, but for some reason they're not.

At many capital equipment companies, pricing just doesn't receive the attention that it deserves, and on those few occasions that the "pricing committee" does meet, the discussion seldom graduates beyond a cost-plus-pricing discussion. This does not constitute a comprehensive pricing strategy.

Optimizing prices requires the same level of attention as cost reduction efforts, and to achieve higher prices, you'll have to get beyond the cost-plus mindset. To get you started, here are six of the best approaches that capital equipment manufacturers can use to improve pricing.

Know Your Value

The price that your product gets has almost nothing to do with its cost. Manufacturers buy capital equipment in hopes of creating more profit. Therefore, price your product based on the value that it creates for the customer. This is almost always the most profitable form of pricing.

Let's say that your product saves the typical customer $1,000,000 a year in operating costs versus the competition's product. You should be able to capture a big part of that savings in the form of a price premium.

The ability to establish value-based pricing is dependent upon your ability to understand how your customer profits from your products. In the case of capital equipment, it means understanding the Value Metric for your product and how it stacks up against the competition. Basically, the Value Metric is the financial expression that describes the additional profit that your customer will make as a result of purchasing your system verses another.

Then your value proposition, expressed in financial terms, must be integrated into your marketing and sales materials. Everything you do in the sales cycle should be focused on reinforcing this value proposition and the unique advantages of your product that deliver it. Constantly repeat and reinforce the amount of cost savings or increased profits that the customer will realize.

Of course, buyers will do everything possible to diminish your value and convince you that low price is the key to winning the business; they are just trying to develop leverage for the negotiation. Don't be thrown by this. If your product really delivers the value and you can substantiate it during the sales process, you'll prevail and secure premium pricing.

Create Frequent Product Extensions

Never let continuous improvements in your product just slide from the engineering lab to your customer's receiving dock. This is often one of the toughest product management tasks. Capital equipment products are constantly changing as a result of changing requirements, response to competitors, refinements to designs, or special requests from customers. Be vigilant about staying on top of product improvements. They take a lot of effort and add value for your customers, so you deserve to get paid for them.

Bundle these improvements into new product extensions. Each of these product extensions brings incremental value and an opportunity to raise prices.

This works best when each extension can be easily adopted by your existing customers without creating an open selection process. An open selection opens the door to a competitive run-off. You don't have to have been in this business very long to realize that pricing never goes in the right direction when that happens. So don't make each extension "too new." It also helps to keep the product name the same, and only change the extension number; for example *RapidWafer I* and *RapidWafer II*.

Create new product extensions every nine to twelve months, and you'll be able to keep your customers buying from you at steadily improving prices.

Make Improvements Available as Upgrades

This obvious but often overlooked move lets you essentially raise prices on systems that you've already sold. Every time you release a new version of your product, make as much of the improvement as possible available to the installed base as an upgrade. Just like systems, these upgrades should be value priced. Furthermore, since there is seldom any competition in the upgrades business, you stand a really good chance of getting your price.

Every upgrade sold increases the total revenue and profit on each system. Think of it this way. Say the original system sold for

$2,000,000 and your profit margin was $800,000. A year later you sell an upgrade for that same system for $300,000 with $180,000 profit margin. The total system price is now $2,300,000, and the total profit margin is now $980,000. By way of the upgrade, you have raised the price 15 percent and increased the profit by 23 percent.

Installed base upgrades will also help you hold prices on new system sales. If you are the incumbent at an account, you can include upgrades for the installed base as part of the new system's package. Since the competition cannot do this, it will be difficult for customers to draw apples to apples comparisons with competing proposals in an effort to drive prices down.

Don't Kill the Old Product

To protect the price of your new product, you need to keep the old product available for a period of time. Price your new product so that it reflects the incremental value. Whenever your customer balks at the price increase, tell them that if price is the issue, you'd be happy to sell them the older model.

This is particularly useful when you are trying to raise pricing with an existing customer. They always want the new product, but they usually aren't willing to pay for it. By keeping the old product around, you'll be in a much better position. You know that the old product will work for them because they are already using it. Therefore, suggesting that they continue to purchase the old product if they have an issue with the new product's pricing is a legitimate position.

If they balk at continuing to buy the old product, take it as a good sign. They are validating that the new product has more value. Make them pay for it.

Create Two Price Points

Even when you have a value advantage, some customers will remain fixated on price. For this reason, always offer a configuration of your product that approximates the value of the competitor's system. Every time the customer insists that you match the competitor's price, just wheel out the stripped-down configuration.

The strategy is the same for old and new versions of the product. If a customer really wants the full performance version, she'll need to step up and pay.

Set Different Prices for Different Customers

From a customer perspective, your product's value is not universal. Some customers will value your product more than others.

Let's say you made a piece of equipment for applications in both microprocessor and memory manufacturing. In the memory application, your performance is about equal to your competitor's performance. But in microprocessors, your system enables higher performance devices. As a result, the microprocessor manufacturer can charge their customers higher prices.

The value proposition is different in different market segments; therefore, the same should go for your prices.

10.Secrets to Successful Product Cost Reduction

Within moments of giving birth to your new product, you were told by senior management to begin reducing its cost.

It means the new product didn't hit its original cost targets; however, that's water over the dam. So your team shifts into "cost-reduction" mode and begins sorting the product's sub-assemblies by their material cost, attacking those at the top of the list. This is a great way to shrink the bill of material, but it doesn't guarantee that the results will make it to the bottom line.

The best time to focus on hitting new product cost goals is during the design phase. Get this right, and you can avoid cost reduction programs altogether. However, if you do find yourself off target on an existing product, you must construct your cost reduction effort to make sure that it will actually result in improved profitability.

Better to Prevent High Costs Than to Reduce Them

Product architecture and design decisions can easily determine more than 80 percent of the final product cost for capital equipment. If that seems a little high, try to recall the last time your organization took more than 20 percent of the cost out of an existing product without a redesign effort. A model for contributors to capital equipment product costs is shown in figure 29.

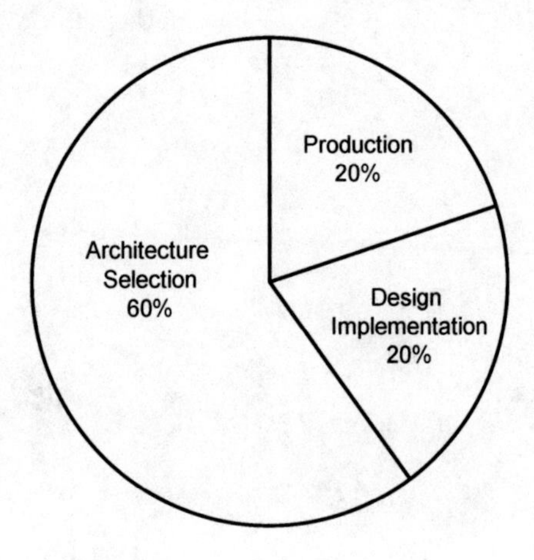

Figure 29: Contributors to Capital Equipment Costs

Your architecture selection locks in more than half of the cost structure. At this stage, you are selecting fundamental technologies and building blocks that will remain with the product over its lifetime. Design implementation, which includes things like material selection, tolerances, and "make-versus-buy" decisions, brings the total design contribution cost up to 80 percent. Production execution on things like yield, fixturing, and supplier selection is only responsible for approximately 20 percent of your total cost.

The bottom line is that decreasing or removing costs is very difficult once products are designed. Capital equipment is just too complex to be "leaned out" during production. So, make the "design to cost" framework a cornerstone of your development process. "Design to cost" is a strategy to treat target costs as an independent design parameter that needs to be achieved during product development. It is a key engineering discipline that warrants a book all its own. However, here are some key "design to cost" tenants worth noting here:

- Explore concept, architecture, and design alternatives for developing lower-cost approaches. There are usually trade-offs between cost and performance; make sure that you look at both.
- Allocate total target cost to the subsystem and component levels of the product structure where costs can be effectively managed. Only describing cost targets at the final product level isn't actionable by the individual design team members. Break costs down to a level at which every design project has a cost target.
- Use documented, revision-controlled design requirements to avoid creeping elegance and feature sets.
- Review and drive development program progress against cost targets as rigorously as you do performance targets. Make sure that every program review looks at both.
- Establish and document design standards to avoid over-engineering finishes and tolerances. Make compliance to standards a criterion for design approval.
- Emphasize common platforms and modularity to drive manufacturing volumes up. The more a part or subsystem is utilized across a product line, the more efficient the development, testing, manufacturing, and servicing will be.
- Don't design new parts when you can buy them off-the-shelf. Off-the-shelf parts save design, documentation, manufacturing, and test costs. Also, suppliers of off-the-shelf parts are more efficient at their specialty, so they can produce the parts at a lower cost.

How to Cost Reduce an Existing Product

If this section applies to you, it means that your "design to cost" efforts didn't go as planned. As discussed already, cost is very difficult to reduce once the product is designed, but that doesn't mean that if you have cost problem, you should give up before trying. Here are some guidelines to help improve your likelihood of success.

1. Make sure that you'll get a return on your investment.

   Usually, cost reduction on existing products involves some level of design change coupled with improvements in supply chain and manufacturing efficiencies. Make sure that the total cost of doing the change will be paid back by the cost savings within the expected life of the product.

Also, watch out for unintended consequences. Sometimes one change can force a cascade of other design changes. All of a sudden, the design effort and associated costs snowball.

2. Never just reduce cost.

   In the high-technology world, performance benchmarks are always rising. Competitive advantages can evaporate if you don't keep investing in performance improvement. It's easy to fall behind if you focus only on cost reduction.

   Let's say you spend a year stripping cost out of your flagship product. At the same time, your competitor works on advancing performance. At the end of that year, your value relative to your competition will be diminished. This means that everything you gained in cost reduction could potentially be given back in price as a result of a weakened position.

   "Cost reduction only" strategies are a lot like treading water. You exert a lot of energy, but you don't get anywhere.

3. Merge cost reduction with performance improvement efforts.

   Instead of just driving cost reduction efforts based on a bill of material sort, merge cost reduction with performance improvement initiatives. Do this by tackling cost reduction as a requirement for every performance improvement project. This is "design for cost" at a continuing engineering or project-by-project level. This way cost reduction comes along for the ride as you advance the product's competitiveness.

   Another benefit of this approach is that it's not necessary to launch individual cost-reduction programs. This reduces both management overhead and resource conflicts.

4. Synchronize cost reduction and performance improvement releases to the market.

   Not only is it best to combine performance and cost improvement efforts, it's imperative that the results be released to market at the same time. If you make a noticeable change to your product that can only be justified to a customer as a cost reduction for you, your cost reduction will quickly become a price reduction and your gross margins will suffer.

   Instead, by bundling cost reduction with performance improvements, you'll score on two fronts. You'll have lowered costs and created the opportunity to increase prices.

Cost Reduction Case Study

This took place at a manufacturer of high-vacuum semiconductor process equipment. The company had been shipping its current-generation product for about a year and had placed it at most of their key customers. Its introduction was considered very successful.

Then came the pressure to reduce its costs.

In response, they changed the product configuration to eliminate one vacuum pump. This change saved tens of thousands of dollars, and extensive testing demonstrated that performance did not degrade. However, the change did not produce any improvement. Since the goal for the program was only cost reduction, that was okay, and they cut the change into the standard bill of materials.

Customers began ordering follow-on systems at about the same time that the new configuration was released. They immediately noticed that their new systems had one less pump. Since the equipment manufacturer couldn't articulate a customer-focused reason for the change, nearly every customer insisted that the missing pump be added or the price be lowered.

The result was that very few systems were sold with the projected gross margins. The manufacturer realized that the cost-reduction project was destined to be a loser if the company didn't do something differently.

The project team brainstormed ideas for recovering the situation. One engineer pointed out that vacuum chamber pump–down time was the throughput bottle neck on the system. By making a small change, they could reduce this time and therefore raise the throughput specification. Plus, the higher throughput could be achieved with the lower-cost, single-pump configuration.

This idea allowed the cost reduction to be bundled with a throughput performance improvement. Customers not only accepted the cost-reduced configuration but, in many cases, paid a premium over their previous purchases.

PART III: MARKETING

1. The Capital Equipment Marketing Mix

The most important part of creating demand for capital equipment products is defining and developing products that address market needs better than the competition does. That's why so much of this book is dedicated to achieving that end. However, even the best-conceived products won't sell themselves. The capital equipment supplier has to develop and deploy a mix of marketing tools and activities that generate demand.

Selecting the best mix of these tools and activities to create demand is directly related to the nature of this market. Capital equipment falls under the umbrella of a discipline referred to as "industrial marketing." This is broadly described as the marketing of goods and services from one business to another. In industrial markets, businesses purchase goods or services in anticipation of using them to generate profit. This is much different from consumer markets, where goods and services are merely consumed.

Capital equipment marketing is a specific category of industrial marketing. It is distinguished by its large transaction sizes, complex buying processes, and the significance of the buying decision on the profitability of the buyer's enterprise. To arrive at an optimal capital equipment marketing mix, you have to fully understand the nature of the customer's business and the essence of his buying process.

The Customer and the Buying Process

It's the nature of the customer, rather than the nature of the product, that distinguishes capital equipment marketing from other disciplines. To optimize your capital equipment marketing mix, you must understand the customer's motivations and expectations.

Capital equipment customers:

- Seek to improve profit through the purchase of capital equipment.
- Are relatively few in number. Often, it is possible to identify all buyers in a particular market segment and therefore engage each with a customized approach.
- Are single organizations in which many people work in teams to select, purchase, and implement capital equipment.
- Expect a long-term relationship with their suppliers.
- Depend on their suppliers to develop an on-going stream of technology advancements.

The best way to sum up these attributes is that the capital equipment customer expects a robust, multi-level relationship with its suppliers. When a customer selects a supplier, she is making a decision that will directly affect the success of her company and likely many careers.

Since the purchase decision has a dynamic impact on the company and individuals, the nature of the selling and buying process is characterized by the following:

- The sales cycle is long. It can take months or more to complete applications development, process qualification, demonstrations, proposals, evaluation periods, and negotiations.

- Selling is one-to-one in nature, and distribution channels are few—most often direct. Therefore, it is relatively easy to build strong relationships.
- Salespeople must be technical problem solvers, utilizing in-depth product and technical knowledge to understand the buyer's needs.
- Transaction dollar values are high enough that they often require board-level approval.
- Purchase decisions are typically made by a team rather than by an individual.
- The decision process is complex. Product specifications, product quality, company reputation, commercial terms, and after-sales service all play into the decision.
- The buying decision process is even more complex when it involves switching from an incumbent supplier to a new one.

With all of these complexities in play, the best marketing mix is one geared toward creating and nurturing a healthy, long-term relationship with the customer.

The Most Effective Marketing Tools

To generate demand from buyers in consumer marketing, the emphasis is on promotion and advertising. Consumers typically do not have a formal purchasing process and are usually not making a mission-critical decision. In fact, the consumer purchasing decision is mostly so inconsequential that advertising alone can be sufficient to close the sale.

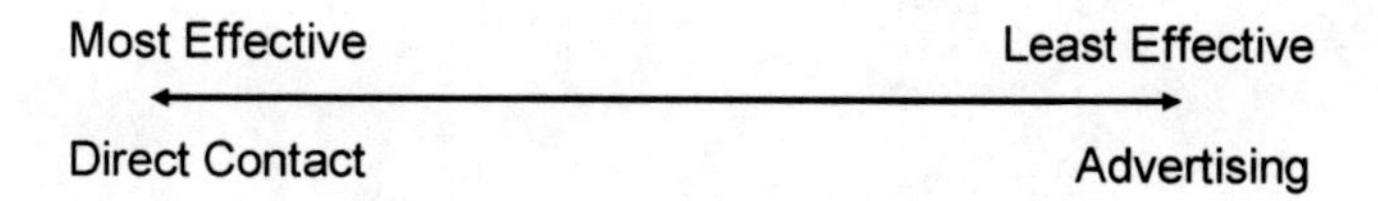

Figure 30: Spectrum of Capital Equipment Marketing Strategies

This is not the case for capital equipment marketing. Instead of advertising and promotion, the most effective tools are those that generate systematic, direct, one-on-one contact with the customer as shown in figure 30.

Here is a list of marketing tools used by capital equipment companies to generate demand and create solid customer relationships grouped according to their effectiveness.

Most effective

- Joint development programs
- User groups
- Technical seminars
- Roadmap and technology exchanges
- Product demonstrations
- Application workshops
- In-person sales presentations

Somewhat effective

- White papers
- Speaking at industry conferences
- Newsletters
- Blogs
- Trade shows

Least effective

- Advertising
- Brochures
- Direct mail
- Public relations
- Non-interactive Web site

All of these marketing tools have a place in the capital equipment marketing mix, but focusing on those in the "most effective" category will produce the best results.

Notice that all the tools in the "most effective" category involve direct contact with the customer. Each creates an exclusive environment where it's just you and the customer over long periods of time. As you move down the list through "somewhat effective" and "least effective," you are moving farther away from direct contact with the customer.

At the bottom of the list are advertising, brochures, public relations, and non-interactive Web sites. These tools can help inform the market about a product or reinforce a company's credibility, but will have minimal direct impact on a purchasing decision. They are best used to support your direct contact marketing efforts, but should never be the cornerstone of a product marketing effort.

Making It All Work

It's a lot easier to generate a brochure, fancy Web site, or an ad than to secure a joint-development agreement with an industry-leading customer. Capital equipment marketing programs are complex and evolve over time.

This complexity means that there's high risk that the customer will receive confusing or conflicting messages about the product or the company selling it. Therefore, the most successful marketing programs:

1. Start way before the product is launched.

   The most important thing is to be perceived as you really are. That's why the process of creating a unique position, and determining with specificity who the customers are and why they buy should be determined before a product development effort even starts.

   Defining a product with a strong value proposition to fuel the engine of the development program will ensure success.

2. Are formally planned and managed

The best marketing programs result from formal planning and management. They systematically select and deploy the most effective marketing tools over extended periods to cement your position in the mind of the customer. The task is too complex and the timeframe too long to approach this in an ad-hoc manner.

3. Stay on message

   It is essential to transmit a simple and well-articulated message consistently across all elements of the marketing arsenal over long periods of time.

   Every marketing effort, whether a joint development program, a speech at a conference, or a one-on-one sales presentation, should connect directly with the market positions that you're taking.

4. Never start with advertising and public relations

   Creative work is fun and exciting, but leading with a promotional campaign is a mistake. First, advertising, public relations, and the like are supporting, not primary, tools for the capital equipment marketer. Second, it's more important to do the hard work of developing a legitimate value proposition and building a marketing program that emphasizes direct contact elements. Do these things first—then writing ad copy will be easy.

The set of marketing activities and tools that you use to generate demand for your goods and services needs to be grounded in a clear position focused on developing long-term customer relationships and addressing the complexities of the capital equipment selling process.

2. Create a Winning Distribution Channel

If the most effective marketing tools develop deep and lasting relationships with your target customers, then the capital equipment supplier must develop a distribution channel that is capable of using those tools.

For capital equipment, this is not easy to do because the products and applications are complex and often rooted deeply in physics, chemistry, and material science. Also, the markets are geographically dispersed and constantly changing. Therefore, many capital equipment companies default to the "factory based" selling model in which the mission of the field sales force is to get a meeting for the factory product expert.

This selling model fundamentally limits the quality of your customer relationships and the scale of your business.

Instead, the capital equipment marketing organization must constantly push product and application knowledge closer and closer to those working in the same time zone and culture of your customers. Only then will you build the kind of relationships that will keep your competitors at bay.

What's Wrong with the Factory-Based Selling Model

Many organizations will argue that high-technology capital equipment is too complex for a field organization to understand. They'll contend that a factory-based product expert, usually holding the title of Product Manager, is needed to lead the sales effort, and the sales force is charged with simply arranging appointments. However, relying on a small group of product experts to drive every sales opportunity creates its own set of issues. Consider these:

- If the only way to win a sale is by the product expert touching it, the bandwidth of this expert becomes the fundamental limitation on revenue growth.
- Since the experts mostly engage customers during an active sales cycle, they never develop the robust relationships that can only come from more frequent and varied interactions.
- Since the local sales force has been reduced to a conduit for factory-based experts, they have little to contribute to the customer relationship. As a result, their relationships remain shallow.
- Product experts who spend all of their time on sales support leave no time to think about creating long-term competitive advantage.
- A competitor with a stronger local presence can easily out maneuver you by operating in real-time while your salesperson waits for a response from the factory expert four time zones away.
- Sales situations can be assessed incorrectly because the factory experts aren't equipped to interpret the subtleties of local culture, organizational dynamics, language, and business practices.

Interestingly enough, it's often the factory experts who perpetuate this situation. They enjoy the attention and recognition that goes with being part of the exclusive "only-one-that-can-make-it-happen" club. To turn this around, you need to redefine the role of these product experts from "sales-doers" to "sales enablers." Doing this will get you more leverage from your distribution channel, resolve the issues above, and foster robust customer relationships.

Roadmap for Best-in-Class Distribution Channel

The objective in distribution-channel development is to put as much selling capability as close to the customer as possible. By localizing product and application expertise, you'll enable the sales force to become a real resource to your customers, and consequently develop meaningful relationships. The sales team that can answer a customer's question in real time rather than say, "I'll ask the factory and get back to you tomorrow," is the sales team that will have the most robust relationships.

Because of the decision-making nature in capital equipment, you'll probably never completely design the factory out of the selling process. Management will always play a role in demonstrating long-term commitments, and product management will likely always support the majority of future product discussions. However, a large portion of the sales support process can be localized. This includes the ability to:

- Position products within each account/region
- Configure the product offering to meet specific customer needs
- Design successful demonstrations
- Prepare and present product presentations
- Draft standard specification responses
- Review product performance data
- Handle objections
- Conduct regional market analysis including competitive information and pricing analysis
- Coordinate and implement local promotion campaigns

Getting to a point where a handful of factory-based experts aren't necessary to directly support the items above can take a long time and, to be candid, may never happen. In some cases, it can be like the elusive "zero defects" quality objective. You're always getting closer to objective but you may never quite get there. This doesn't mean that the objective is invalid; it just means that you have to apply a consistent and persistent effort to keep moving toward the goal of field self-sufficiency. The goal should be one of continuous improvement and not one of "hit the goal and be done."

It's the responsibility of the marketing organization to drive constant progress toward localizing selling capability. Almost all high-technology capital equipment companies start out with a heavy reliance on factory-based experts to execute the sales process, and, over time, the best ones localize more and more of that capability. To do this, you'll need a roadmap like the one in figure 31. This roadmap describes the three distinct distribution channel development phases through which you must progress in order to localize your selling capability.

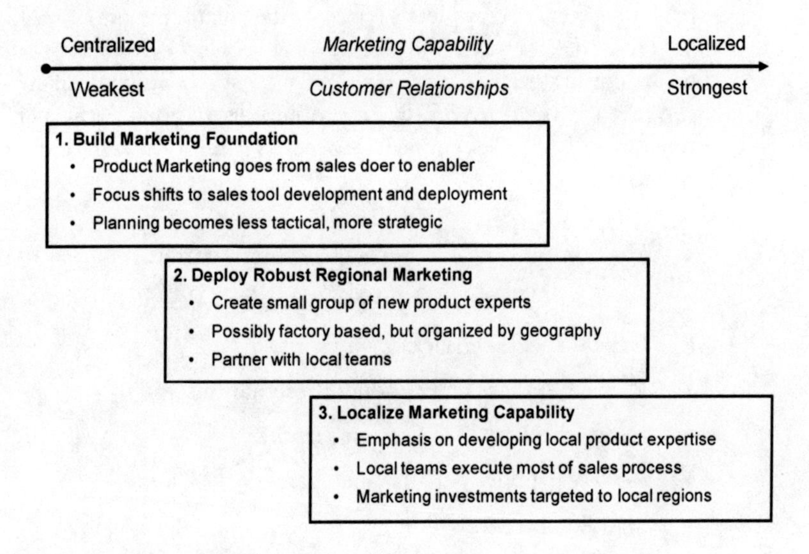

Figure 31: Distribution Channel Development Roadmap

In the first phase, the emphasis is on creating the sales toolkit that will ultimately be deployed to local sales teams. It's here that the mindset shifts from developing a selling tool that addresses a specific sales issue to a robust sales toolkit that supports a variety of selling situations. This requires that more thought be put into to articulating your positions and value proposition. It also demands that the sales materials, such as sales presentations, reach higher levels of professionalism and clarity. No longer are the latest and greatest presentations living somewhere on the product expert's laptop. In this phase, selling materials are peer reviewed, optimized, and posted in a central repository for others to use. You are in essence institutionalizing the knowledge of the product expert in preparation to transfer it to the field.

In the second phase, you are creating the first new set of product experts to support the sales process. Often this is a factory-based organization with the title "regional marketing" or "regional business development." They are organized to reflect the topography of your market (often regionally, or perhaps by product application) with a charter to provide first-level technical sales support. They must be armed with the tools and training that you developed in phase one so that they are capable of carrying a significant portion of the technical sales support load. Because this new tier of product experts is focused on specific customer groups, they advance the cause of developing deeper customer relationships.

By the time you get to phase three, the regional marketing team's ability to provide technical sales support is almost indistinguishable from that of the product manager. Here their focus shifts from "doer" to "enabler," and they begin to emphasize developing local selling capability. The objective is to hire and develop local resources who can execute the majority of the selling cycle without relying on direct contact from factory experts. As the organization continues to grow, increases in marketing and technical selling headcount are focused on the local regions as opposed to expanding the factory organization.

Think of this distribution channel development model like a franchise business model. With a franchise, headquarters is responsible for developing the processes, infrastructure, and tools to enable the franchisees to sell their products in their local markets. Headquarters spends more time working on the problem of creating sustainable demand than on individual transactions. Also, as the franchise grows, most of the new resources are added at the franchisee, not franchisor, level. The franchise business model was developed to create a highly leveraged distribution channel for good products. While not a perfect metaphor for capital equipment distribution, the general concepts apply.

How to Implement the Distribution Channel Roadmap

The distributed selling capability model assumes a decent size enterprise. To truly develop a localized selling capability for capital equipment requires a local arsenal of product and applications specialists in each local market. This is not practical for a small organization. On the other hand, if you don't push your organization toward localizing selling capability, you'll never grow past being a small enterprise.

That's why the capital equipment supplier needs to think in terms of a distribution channel development roadmap. Your strategy is to always move your organization toward localized selling capability. Your action plan needs to follow these three steps.

1. Determine where you stand against the capital equipment distribution channel development roadmap.
2. Define, plan, and execute the next most important steps to become more localized.
3. Go back to step one and repeat for continuous improvement.

Even if you never fully localize your selling capability, there's tremendous value in just making consistent and persistent progress. Your local sales and applications teams will develop strong multi-dimensional customer relationships, and your product experts will have more time to develop and implement product strategies to create competitive advantage.

3. Rock Solid Product Positions Don't Just Happen

Your success in a market depends on how much better you establish your product position versus your competitors. This would be easy if all you had to do was figure out how to communicate your product's key features and benefits, coin a clever slogan, and buy advertising.

But, it's not that easy.

You have to understand and communicate your product's specific differences and how those differences deliver value better than the competitions' products. Then you have to cement that position throughout your market. If you master this process, you can define the competitive landscape and drive the competition to spend all their time defending themselves against the positions that you've established.

Four Capital Equipment Product Positioning Rules

A product position is defined as the unique place your product occupies in the mind of your customer. The goal is to make that position so effective that it compels that customer to make purchasing decisions in your favor.

It's important to note that creating positions for capital equipment is a lot different than creating positions for consumer goods. With consumer goods, buyers are not typically very interested in detailed performance comparisons when selecting products, nor do they take the time to assess them. As a result, positioning consumer goods on intangibles such as industry leadership, quality, and service can be very effective.

However, in the world of capital equipment, buyer behavior is different. Here buyers are buying to maximize profit, and suppliers are evaluated on their ability to help them do it. Their buying processes are formal and analytical. Multiple suppliers are often evaluated side by side through demonstrations and performance data reviews. Several capital equipment markets even have formal cost of ownership models that standardize the evaluation criteria.

This doesn't mean that you should ignore intangibles when positioning. It does mean, however, that you must connect your position directly to your value proposition and then prove it.

The good news is you only need to follow four simple rules to define effective product positions for capital equipment. Your product positions must be:

1. True
2. Unique
3. Directly connected to your value proposition
4. Important to the buying decision

Let's take a look at each of these:

1. True

In capital equipment, the purchasing process is very formal, and you can expect to be asked for data and to conduct live demonstrations to prove your claims. Empty claims are quickly exposed.

2. Unique

   By definition, a position is the unique place that you occupy in the market relative to your competitors. If you can attribute your position to a specific product feature that your competition doesn't have and cannot imitate, you passed the "unique" test. This could be related to architecture, technology, or process.

3. Directly connected to your value proposition

   At the end of the day, what matters is creating financial value. You need to be able to draw a direct connection between your position and a unique ability to make profit for your customers.

4. Important to the buying decision

   Ultimately, you want your product position to lead to purchases. Therefore, the positions that you take must directly impact factors that are important to the buying decision. For example, positioning on a unique ability to achieve high production yields is likely a more effective position than touting the quality of your user documentation.

Crafting the Positioning Statement

Once your position passes the four rules, it's time to think about crafting a message that will resonate with your customers, often called a positioning statement. This handful of words forms the fountain from which all of your product marketing activities flow, so it's important to spend the time to get it right.

Every good positioning statement contains these key elements:

- Value proposition
- Target market

- 2–4 positions with your unique benefit and the unique product feature that delivers it

Here is a sample positioning statement for a fictional thin film deposition system used to make solar cells. The equipment manufacturer is putting forward a lower manufacturing costs value proposition, pinned to its unique ability to deliver the highest throughput, longest maintenance-free production runs, and highest yields.

TurboFilm XT lowers thin film solar cell manufacturing[1] *costs by 30 percent*[2] *Its…*

- *High-power microwave source produces the fastest deposition rates for highest throughput*[3]
- *Self-cleaning process chamber enables the longest production runs between maintenance events*[4]
- *In-situ closed-loop process control ensures the highest yields*[5]

Take a look at the superscripted footnotes on the positioning statement above. They correspond to each of the key elements of the positioning statement as follows:

1. Target market
2. Value proposition
3. Position #1
4. Position #2
5. Position #3

This positioning statement does much more than make advantage claims. It also establishes the competitive issues for products like the fictional *TurboFilm XT*. It advocates that the way to measure value is by measuring manufacturing costs and goes further to define the most important factors in achieving that value: throughput, uninterrupted production, and yield. A good positioning statement establishes the rules of the game, and if you write the rules, you're more likely to win.

The sample positioning statement is also precise and concise. The definition of value is clear, as are the key advantages and the features of the product that deliver them. If you are too vague, your message will sound like baseless claims, if it is too long, your message will get lost.

To test your positioning statement, imagine bumping into the CEO of your customer's company. He asks you to explain, in fifty words or less, why he should buy your product. If your positioning statement does the job convincingly, you pass the test.

How to Refer to the Competition

Since a position is always relative to competitive offerings, you have to refer to the competition in your marketing efforts. This can be a delicate situation and is all about striking the right balance.

You will need to be very specific about the differences between you and your competitors when making your case to customers. But at the same time, you'll be selling in environments where direct "competitor bashing" is not appropriate. Every situation and market will differ, but there are three principles that you can use to guide the development of your marketing materials and campaigns that will allow you to be aggressive without being offensive.

1. Draw direct product comparisons.

   If you are attributing your unique value to a feature, you need to directly point out that your competitor doesn't have the feature or has chosen an inferior design. Don't rely on your customer to figure it out.

2. Never refer to your competitor by name.

   Use terms like, "Product A," "Alternative Approach," or "Competitor B." It's a classier way to draw the comparison, and by not using their name you're not improving their brand recognition.

3. Use the "design considerations" approach.

Still bring up the differences between you and your competitor, but treat your competitor's approaches as alternatives that you considered but rejected. Take your customer down a path highlighting the flaws in all the approaches except yours.

Cementing Your Position

Figuring out what your position is and how to express it is actually the easy part. The tough work comes in cementing your position in the market. This means that you have established your advantage and value and set the ground rules for evaluating the performance and value of products like yours. You'll know that you are cemented in the market when you observe the following:

- Customers' purchasing specifications and selection processes reflect the issues that you've established in your positioning. For example, if you positioned "deposition rates" as important to product performance, you know that it's working if customer purchasing specifications include it and give it a heavy weighting in the selection criteria.
- There are signs that your competitors are being forced to play on the competitive playing field that you've established. Signs include roadmap commitments to implement features like yours and presentations that spend more time defending against your positions instead of establishing their own.
- Third parties in the industry infrastructure such as industry analyst and trade publication editors are echoing your version of what constitutes value and important product capabilities.
- Your trademark name for your unique feature becomes your industry's generic reference, like Band-Aid®, Kleenex®, or Xerox®.

There are only two key principles that you need to remember when it comes to establishing your position in the market. They are:

1. Establish credibility
2. Use multiples channels, but broadcast just one message

If there's one thing that will kill a good position, it's a market that doesn't believe it's true. If this happens, a position is viewed as nothing more than an empty slogan. Since buyers of capital equipment are skeptical by nature, they'll need a lot of convincing that you are really as good as you say. Credibility comes from assembling irrefutable evidence that your positions are true and will translate into profit for your customer. To establish this credibility you need to:

1. Obtain references

   Nothing builds credibility better than having someone else validate your claims, and there's no better validation than having the right customer as a reference. These references can be direct—where your customer will tell others about your product's performance, or inferred—when it becomes known in your industry that certain customers are buying your product.

   When it comes to references, not all customers are created equal. For a reference to influence buying behavior, the customer must be well respected. A reference from an obscure start-up just won't have the gravitas to sway industry titans to consider your offering. In some capital equipment segments, there's a whole tier of buyers that watch what the leaders buy and duplicate their decisions because they know that the selection process of these leaders is more rigorous than their own could ever be. That's why it's important, especially early in the life of a product, to secure an influential lead customer.

2. Provide data, data, and more data

   Not long after you've made your first pitch positioning the advantages of your product, you are going to be asked to prove it with data. That means you need to have a combination of data from field performance and tests that you have conducted.

   You'll need a library of data that confirms your advantages as well as data for other important performance metrics so that customers can also verify that you don't have any performance defects. The most important thing is to have data collected under the same conditions that reflect your customers' environments so that the data is viewed in a similar context.

3. Never fail a customer demo

   The final step in establishing credibility is the product demonstration. Eventually, after learning of other manufacturers using your system and reviewing the data with which you have provided them, customers are going to want to test it for themselves.

   Nothing will damage your credibility faster than a failed demo. Customers expect that a demonstration is a highly orchestrated event, and any failure in a tightly controlled environment indicates potential disaster in the real world. Because of this, demonstrations are a high-risk step in the selling process.

   To improve your odds of success, you'll need to make sure that you have agreement with the customer on a detailed demonstration plan, and always have a pristine demo system with a trained demo team ready to go.

The next thing you need to do to cement your position is to make sure that your message is getting out through every possible channel in your market infrastructure. These channels potentially include:

- Customer presentations
- Marketing materials
- Industry conferences
- Sales and technical training
- Customer seminars
- Industry publications
- Investor conference calls
- Social media outlets
- Press releases
- Tradeshows

What's critical is that every channel gets the same message. Your target market gets bombarded with hundreds, if not thousands of marketing messages a day. To make yours stick, you have to be relentless in your consistency.

To get this consistency, you need to leverage all of your marketing channels:

1. Build presentation sales kits that allow you to sustain a sales cycle on your definition of the competitive issues and your advantages.

   Always have that next level of detail when the customer says, "I don't believe you; prove it" or "That's an intriguing advantage. Can you come back next week and present more information?" The more weapons your sales kit contains to support your positions, the longer you can keep the sales process focused on your definition of the competitive issues and your advantages.

2. Make sure that your contributions to technical conferences and publications support your positions.

   The best way to do this is to have the marketing team examine the conference and trade publication editorial schedule for your industry and identify opportunities that would reinforce your positioning. Then create a list of topics that will support your position and submit it to your company's technical community to conduct the study, then develop and submit content.

   Industry conferences and publications are very valuable channels for establishing the credibility of your positions. Don't let your technical community run open-loop on topic selection or submission content.

3. Integrate investor and customer messaging

   What you say to investors and customers needs to be consistent. This can be tricky, since you may want to let investors know that your market leadership enables you to charge higher prices, but you want your customers to credit you for helping to lower their costs. Both may be true, but the messaging is all wrong. A customer hearing how you talk to investors about your high prices will think that you are disingenuous when you say that you're focused on lowering their costs.

So find words and phrases that work for both investors and customers. Instead of "high prices" to investors and "lower costs" to customers, use a phrase like "highest value" for both. You can test your approach by taking your investor presentation and imagine that you are presenting it to a customer. Then ask yourself, "Does the presentation help or hurt my position in the market?"

4. Get it right, then don't change frequently

   Establish your positioning and its communication thoroughly, and then stick with it. Changing frequently is confusing to your market and will prevent your message from having any staying power.

   From the equipment supplier point of view, this will feel like you are just saying the same thing over and over again. You are, but bear in mind that that's not how your market perceives it. You are competing with a lot of "noise," so it takes repeated exposure to your message in order for it to stick in your customer's mind. Every time you change your message, you hit the reset button.

Establishing a rock solid position requires a position that is true, unique, and connected to your value proposition and to your customers' buying decision. The articulation of that position must be concise and precise. Finally, to cement your position in the market, you must communicate consistently across the entire market infrastructure.

4. Anatomy of the Capital Equipment Sales Kit

The custom nature of every sales situation in high-technology capital equipment makes the notion of a standard sales kit seem like a fantasy. Each customer has his own special requirements and views the issues differently. A traditional, fully-scripted "sales pitch pack" will most certainly miss the mark and have customers feeling that you are insensitive to their needs.

At the same time, these markets are competitive, the products are complex, and the customers are sophisticated. So, developing sales and marketing materials on the fly isn't likely to produce a clear picture of your value and advantages. If you haphazardly create your selling materials in response to requests for information or your competitor's latest assault, you'll fail to get your message across.

Developing a set of standard sales and marketing materials for capital equipment has its unique challenges. You need to develop tools that allow you to sustain a full sales cycle on the product positions and competitive issues that you want to be driving the buying decision. This sales kit needs to be structured to support each stage of the selling process, and at the same time, it needs to be configurable to conform to the unique requirements of each customer.

Why You Need a Standard Sales Kit

Perhaps you think the standardization of a sales kit is a waste of effort because every selling situation is different. However, you really need to think about the consequences of an ad-hoc approach. A lot can go wrong.

- Selling price is always going to be an issue. Your ability to keep your margins intact is dependent on your ability to prove and reinforce your unique value at every step in the sales process. You can't count on an ad-hoc set of presentation slides packed with random features and benefits to get you there.
- If you haven't fully locked down your selling specifications and ensured consistency with your selling materials, you risk over committing, which will lead to customer dissatisfaction and potential revenue recognition issues.
- Without a thoroughly developed and supported "story," you'll default to tactically answering customer requests for information or responding to issues established by your competitors. You'll spend the whole sales cycle "fetching rocks," instead of getting your value and position established. This is good for the competition but not for you.
- Against a competitor who has orchestrated a flawless sales cycle, you will appear amateurish. It would be like showing up for the Super Bowl without practicing and without a playbook. There would be lots of effort and creativity on the field, but no coordinated effort and no chance of winning.
- You'll lose control of your message. You'll be at the mercy of anyone touching the sale to position the issues however they want. This can no doubt lead to countless mistakes, retractions, and even losing the order.
- Without a grab-n-go set of materials, you'll be caught flat footed when you're asked to make a presentation to a customer who just arrived in your lobby unannounced.

A standard sales kit enables you to create a fully integrated set of materials designed to seamlessly support your value and ability to deliver it. It ensures that no matter where the selling is happening, it's consistent with what the best minds in your company have determined will work. It's the foundation from which you train sales and field marketing personnel to articulate your "story," making the sales process less dependent on a few factory experts.

Structure of a Capital Equipment Sales Kit

A capital equipment sales kit needs to cover the entire sales cycle from prospecting to purchase order. You can think of this kit much in the same way as you think of the bill of materials for a piece of capital equipment. At the highest level is the parent assembly, beneath which are all of its supporting elements. Figure 32 shows the primary elements of the sales kit concept.

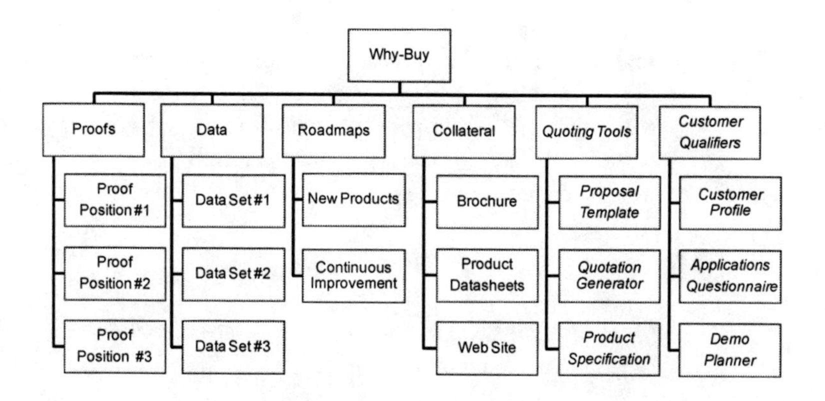

Figure 32: Capital Equipment Sales Kit Concept

At the top of the sales kit is the Why-Buy presentation. It's the ten to fifteen slides that make the case for purchasing your product over competitor offerings, and it contains your most concise articulation of your positioning and value proposition. If you had twenty minutes with the CEO at your target customer, this is the presentation that you would use.

The Why-Buy presentation sits at the top of the sales kit bill of materials for precisely the same reason that the top-level assembly sits on top of your product's bill of materials. Everything below it must directly support it. In the case of the sales kit, six subcategories of sales and marketing materials support the arguments made in the Why-Buy presentation. The sales kit bill of material subcategories are:

1. Proofs

   Proof presentations are the next level of detail for each of the positions that you took in the Why-Buy presentation. For example, if one of your positions was having the highest throughput, then you'd have a proof presentation with ten to twenty slides making a detailed case for your unique capability to deliver high throughput. If you took three positions in your "Why Buy" presentation, then you would have three stand-alone proof presentations.

   The proof presentation is there to respond to the customer who says, "I'm interested in learning more about your throughput," or "High throughput is important to us. I just don't believe you can really deliver." The proof presentation is that next level of detail to keep the sales process moving and focused on the positions that you're establishing.

2. Data

   One of the keys to establishing a credible position is having performance data to support it.

   The data portion of the sales kit is organized around performance areas such as throughput, yield, and reliability. Each data pack is a collection of stand-alone slides that contain the data, test conditions, and a headline stating the conclusion that you want the customer to reach.

   In addition to data packs to support the positions that you are taking, include other performance areas that are likely to be examined in the sales process.

3. Roadmaps

These are the official external versions of your future product plans. Capital equipment buyers expect a long-term relationship with their supplier and a steady stream of technical advances. These are the tools to address that expectation. You'll need to keep two roadmaps: one to address questions about future products, and one to address inquiries about continuous improvement for the installed base.

Remember, these roadmaps should reinforce the positions that you're taking. So again, if you've positioned on throughput, your roadmaps should show how your company will continue investing to sustain that advantage.

4. Collateral

   This is the collection of media that gets distributed to customers during the sales process. It includes items such as brochures and datasheets plus virtual materials such as the product page on your company's Web site and any associated social media. Again, all of this must echo and reinforce the product's positioning.

5. Quoting Tools

   Everything that you need to configure and quote your product goes here. Example items that you might include are product configurators, price lists, product specifications, and proposal templates.

6. Customer Qualifiers

   You want sales to find customers that fit your target market. You'll need to understand their particular needs, and, if and when they come in for a demo, you'll want to be sure that it's successful. All of the tools to qualify prospects, clarify the specifics of their application, and define the scope for demonstrations go here.

The sales kit concept also describes two broad subcategories: those items that can be shared with customers and those that cannot. "Why-Buy," Proofs, Data, Roadmaps, and Collateral are designed to be shared with customers. Quoting and Customer Qualifier tools are for internal use only.

Sales Cycle vs. Sales Kit Elements

If the purpose of a sales kit is to support a selling process focused on the competitive issues as you've defined them, then it's important to be able to map the tools in your sales kit to the capital equipment sales cycle. The sales cycle can be described in five phases.

1. Prospect
2. Qualify
3. Create Value
4. Propose
5. Close

Figure 33 shows the individual sales tools in the sales kit and their relationship to the phases in the sales cycle.

Phase	Prospect	Qualify	Create Value	Propose	Close
Sales Kit Tools	Brochure Datasheets Website	Customer Profile Applications Questionnaire	Why-Buy Presentation Proof Presentations Data Roadmaps Demonstration Planner	Product Specifications Proposal Template Quotation Generator	Proposal and Quotation

Figure 33: Sales Kit Mapped against the Sales Cycle

Notice that more tools are focused on the "Create Value" phase than on any other part of the cycle. That's because it's the most important. If you cannot create value in the mind of the customer, you're facing a brutal price and terms battle in the closing phase, or even worse, you may lose the deal. The decision to buy is actually made in this part of the sales cycle. If you create value, the proposal and closing phases become a formality.

The Presentation Deck of Cards

Now it's time to address the seemingly conflicting requirement of creating and using a standard sales kit and to address a market in which each customer has unique requirements and buying processes.

To explain the approach, we're going to use the metaphor of a deck of cards. In a card game, cards can be selected from a deck to produce countless different hands. The definition of "a good hand" varies depending on the game that you're playing.

The same concept works with the sales kit. In this case, the sales kit is your deck of cards, and the game you are playing is your specific sales situation. Figure 34 shows the three steps to creating a winning hand from your presentation deck of cards.

1. Assess the sales situation
2. Review sales kit materials
3. Select materials to match sales situation

Issues
Needs
Competition

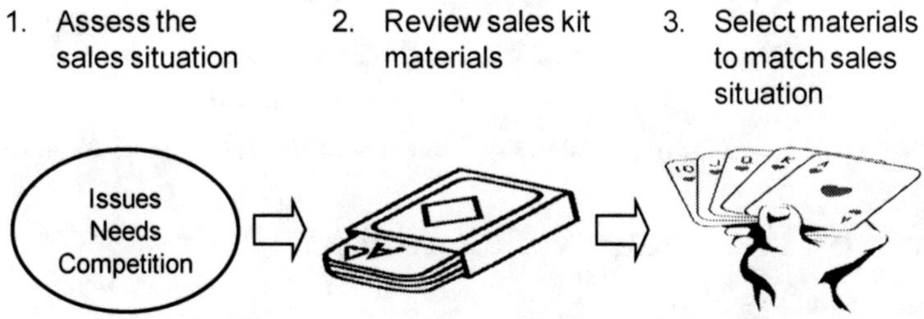

Figure 34: Steps to Using the Sales Kit as a Deck of Cards

For example, let's say that a prospect has asked your company to make a product presentation. Your efforts in the qualifying phase produced the insight that this prospect is focused on reliability performance. That's good, because in addition to "Fastest Throughput" and "Shortest Setup Time," "Highest Reliability" is one of the positions that you take.

Given your prospect's focus on reliability, you'd take your "Why-Buy" presentation and supplement it with several slides from your reliability proof presentation and several slides from your reliability data sets. Now you've got a winning deck of slides.

To make this work, the sales kit needs to be built with the "deck of cards" concept in mind. All of the slides from the Why-Buy, Proof, Data, and Roadmap materials must have a common look and feel so that they can be mixed and matched and not look like they came from different companies. See figure 35.

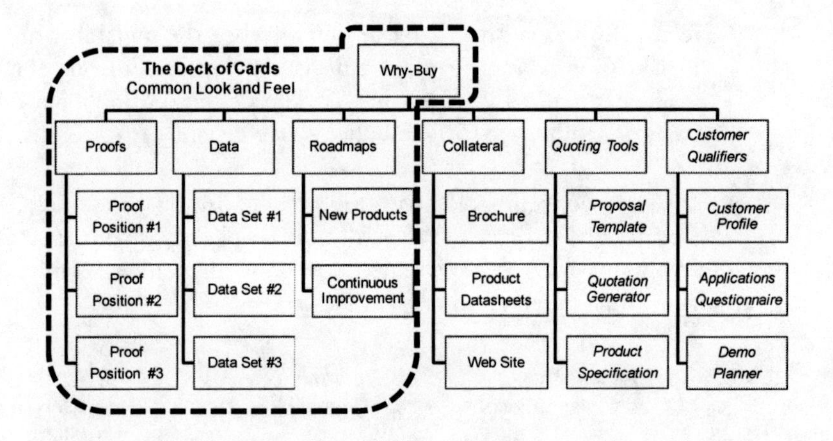

Figure 35: Sales Kit with Deck of Cards Elements Highlighted

Role of Field Sales vs. Factory Marketing

Field sales and factory marketing have distinct roles when it comes to employing the sales kit to address a sales situation. The two organizations need to work together to win.

The marketing organization's role is to:

- Articulate the product's value and position
- Understand the competition
- Create a comprehensive sales kit
- Train sales on sales kit usage
- Cover for gaps in sales kit

The sales organization's role is to:

- Understand customer needs
- Understand the sales situation
- Customize sales kit materials to address the sales situation
- Identify gaps in the sales kit and ask marketing for help

You can see that the sales kit concept fully supports the notion of factory marketing in a sales enabler role, and it positions sales to add value and be a true product consultant to the customer.

It's not a contradiction of terms to say "standard sales kit" and "capital equipment selling" in the same sentence. However, to be successful, you'll need to structure sales kits to support each stage of the selling process, and make sure that they can be shuffled to create a winning hand for a broad scope of selling situations.

5. Simple Formula for Writing the Why-Buy Presentation

The most important part of your capital equipment sales kit is the Why-Buy presentation. These slides tell your value story, and they set the framework for everything else in your marketing arsenal. So, you need to get it right.

Unfortunately, Why-Buy presentations are usually poorly constructed—or worse, they never get developed. Instead, many companies live with a collection of product feature and benefit slides, but these slides never answer the most important question, "Why should I buy your product?" Ask your sales team, and they'll tell you that they can't be successful without a concise answer to that question. The purpose of this chapter is to help you create this vital cornerstone of your sales kit.

First, Think Differently

We usually think of product overview presentations as a summary of key features and benefits because it feels natural to organize them this way. These presentations actually do a fine job of educating your customer about the key capabilities of your product.

The problem is that this leads to a presentation organized much like a tour through an art museum. You walk your customer through the system architecture pointing out key features along the way, just like an art museum tour guide educates visitors about the paintings on the wall. The result is similar as well. After a museum tour, you know a lot more about the paintings but feel no compulsion to purchase the museum. A product presentation organized in the features-and-benefits tour format educates the customers, but doesn't motivate them to buy.

Your job as a marketer is to sell your solution, not to educate your customer. The Why-Buy presentation needs to be organized around the customer's problem and your unique ability to solve it. It starts with framing the problem that you are solving, conveying your unique ability to solve it, and finally, connecting your unique solution to the financial value that it has for the customer. The distinction between a typical product overview and a well constructed Why-Buy presentation is shown in figure 36.

Typical Product Overview	**Why-Buy Presentation**
Educate Feature/Benefit	Sell Problem/Solution

Figure 36: Typical Product Overview vs. Why-Buy Presentation

Why-Buy Presentation Flow

The Why-Buy presentation makes the case for buying your product by accomplishing these three things in this order:

1. Makes the problem-solution connection
2. Establishes unique ability to deliver that solution
3. Translates your unique ability into customer value

This can typically be achieved with a total of 10–15 slides using the framework shown in table 15.

Table 15: Why-Buy Presentation Flow, Sections, and Slide Count

Section	Number of Slides
1. Industry Challenge	1
2. Implications for Your Product Type	1
3. Positioning Statement	1
4. Position Proofs	2 per position
5. Comparative Financials	1–2
6. Positioning Statement (Repeat)	1
Total	10–15

Using the flow above, a Why-Buy presentation that takes three positions could have as few as eleven slides. Let's take a look at each of the elements of the Why-Buy presentation in more detail.

Connecting Problem to Solution

The first three slides create a direct connection from the industry problem to your solution. This three-step process entails first stating the industry problem, then its implications for products like yours, and finally how you uniquely address the implications.

To illustrate this concept, let's walk through a hypothetical example of how a supplier of thin film deposition equipment for the solar cell industry might connect the industry problem to its unique ability to provide a solution. See the three slide sequence in figure 37.

Notice that these three slides have line-by-line alignment. There's no mistaking that the high-power microwave source provides maximum throughput to address the industry problem of deploying productive factories. When constructing your own Why-Buy presentation, you'll want to achieve the same obvious problem-solution connection.

Industry Challenge

Solar cell manufacturers must constantly lower costs by:

- Deploying very productive factories
- Maximizing capital equipment utilization
- Achieving high production yields

Implications For Deposition System Suppliers

To contribute to lowering manufacturing costs, deposition system suppliers must:

- Maximize system throughput
- Minimize downtime due to maintenance
- Consistently operate in tight process windows

TurboFilm XT Advantage

TurboFilm XT lowers solar cell manufacturing costs 30%:

- High-power microwave source produces the fastest deposition rates for highest throughput
- Self cleaning process chamber enables the longest production runs between maintenance events
- In-situ closed loop process control ensures the highest yields

Figure 37: Slides to Connect Problem and Solution in Why-Buy Presentation

If you find this difficult, try creating a worksheet like the one in figure 38 before you build your presentation. You can start anywhere in the worksheet, just make sure that you can make the challenge-implication-advantage link for each position.

Challenge	Implication	Advantage
Deploying very productive factories	Maximize system throughput	High-power microwave source produces the fastest deposition rates for highest throughput
Maximizing capital equipment utilization	Minimize downtime due to maintenance	Self cleaning process chamber enables the longest production runs between maintenance events
Achieving high production yields	Consistently operate in tight process windows	In-situ closed loop process control ensures the highest yields

Figure 38: Challenge-Implication-Advantage Link Worksheet

This careful construction of the problem-solution connection takes the customer down this thought process:

1. You understand my problem.
2. You understand what you're supposed to do about it.
3. You do it.

Making this clear problem-solution connection establishes the importance of your solution to the customer, makes them receptive to hearing more, and gives context for your unique value.

Establishing Unique Ability to Deliver the Solution

It may be tempting in this section to fall back into a feature-benefit tour approach, but don't do it. Here you are establishing that each position in your "Advantage" slide is unique and true. This is accomplished with only two slides for each position. The first slide establishes the source of your advantage, and the second provides the data to prove it.

The first of these two slides establishes your solution as unique by comparing your approach to your competitor's approach. It's not enough to just describe your solution. You need to draw direct, side-by-side comparisons of your superior solution to that of the competitor. Remember, your objective is not to educate the customer; it's to convince him to buy your solution. You need to draw direct comparisons and not assume that the customer will figure it out the important differences on his own.

The second slide contains representative performance data supporting your claim. Whenever possible, show data that compares your performance to that of your competitor. The best data is always that from real customers showing head-to-head competition in a production environment. A reasonable substitute is customer data for your product with the competitor's specification overlaid.

In this section of your Why-Buy presentation, work really hard to create the most concise and clear evidence that your advantages are unique and demonstrable. On each slide, stay on message and don't add extraneous facts, data, or figures, as they will only distract your audience. Continuing with our hypothetical example, the two slides in figure 39 "prove" that *TurboFilm XT* has the unique ability to deliver system throughput.

Comparative Financials

Remember, value is a financial expression, and the only reason why organizations buy capital equipment is to make a profit. So this is the money shot where you tie it all together and describe your value in financial terms.

Here are a few guidelines for developing comparative financials.

1. Always create a direct comparison with your competition.
2. Keep the analysis to those factors established in your product positions.
3. Use system prices for your product that would thrill your CEO if you could actually get them.
4. Make sure that your analysis and the data stand up to scrutiny.

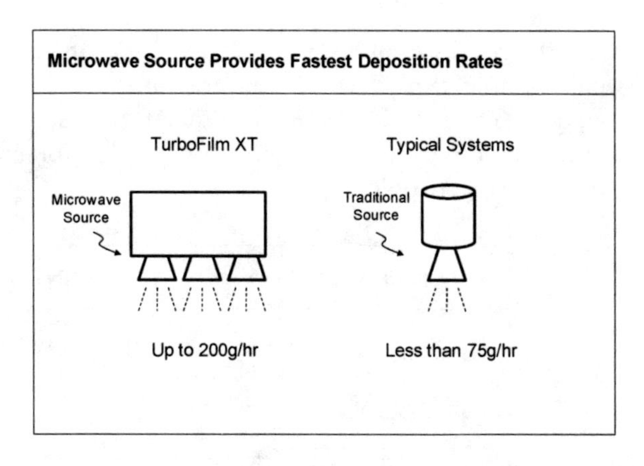

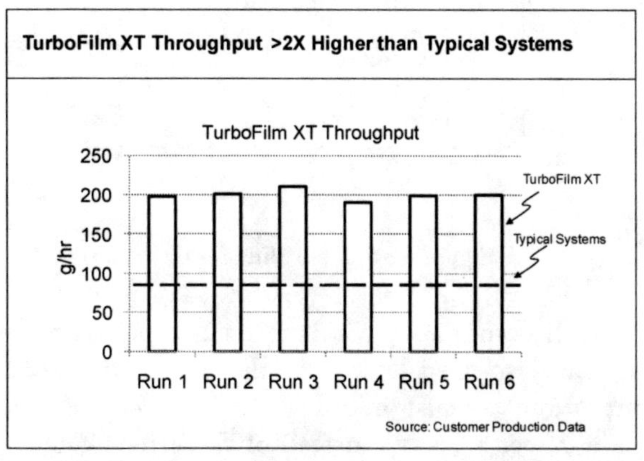

Figure 39: Two Slides to Establish Unique Ability to Deliver the Solution

To illustrate how to present comparative financials, let's turn again to our *TurboFilm XT* example. The *TurboFilm XT* is positioned on highest throughput, longest productive time without maintenance, and highest yield. So our comparative financials need to relate those advantages directly to increased profit for the customer. See sample slide in figure 40.

Notice that in our example we have only factored in the financial parameters affected by the example's positioning (throughput, downtime, and yield). Your first reaction might be that this is over simplified and doesn't account for all costs associated with manufacturing solar cells. This is true, but that's precisely the point. Your customer may initially have the same reaction and point out that you left out facility, utility, raw materials, and other costs. To that, you would simply say, "Those costs are essentially the same across all suppliers. They are important in order to calculate absolute cost of ownership; however, they aren't that helpful for choosing between two equipment suppliers."

TurboFilm XT Lowers Manufacturing Costs by >30%

	TurboFilm XT	Typical Systems
Maximum Deposition Rate (g/hr)	200	75
Grams/Solar cell	5	5
Maximum Solar Cells/Hour	40	15
Maximum Solar Cells/Year	350,400	131,400
System Downtime(Maintenance)	5%	10%
Adjusted Solar Cells/Year	332,880	118,260
Solar Cell Yield	98%	92%
Good Solar Cells/Year	326,222	108,799
System Price	5,000,000	2,500,000
System Depreciation Expense/Yr	1,000,000	400,000
Cost/Solar Cell	**$3.07**	**$4.60**

Figure 40: Sample Slide for Comparative Financials

Another common reaction from customers is to correct a number in your analysis. Usually it's one that relates directly to their process. In our example, a customer may say that they use 10 grams of deposited material per solar cell instead of 5. Perfect! They are now engaged in the construction of your argument and helping you to get your financial model to match their process. Your response is to change the 5 to a 10. The new costs are now $6.13/cell for *TurboFilm XT* and $9.19/cell for typical systems. It's a different set of numbers, but it's the same conclusion.

Finally, notice that when you construct your value argument though comparative financials, you can immediately establish the expectation that your system will cost more. Our example is probably a little extreme, but we've shown a 30 percent cost advantage at twice the system price.

Take the time to create an effective Why-Buy presentation, as it forms the cornerstone of your sales kit and is far more effective than the features and benefits tour format for compelling a customer to buy your product.

6. How to Manage and Acquire Competitive Intelligence

When positioning products, it's important to use direct and specific comparisons to your competitors. It follows that you'll need an effective system for managing and acquiring competitive intelligence.

Collecting intelligence is like a scavenger hunt. Nuggets of information are hidden everywhere. Your challenge is to go out and find them. But the hunt cannot be conducted as random bursts of effort if you want to develop truly effective competitive intelligence. In a world where the competitive environment is constantly evolving, ad-hoc approaches will never develop and maintain a comprehensive profile of the competition. To keep up, you'll need a methodical, disciplined approach to ensure that you always have a handle on what your competitors are doing.

Before you can put your competitive intelligence management and acquisition system into action, you'll need to understand:

1. What you need to know
2. Where to go to get it

3. Who does what

With this framework, you'll be ready to develop and deploy your system to tie it all together and ensure a rigorous, dependable process.

What You Need to Know

Competitive intelligence can be broken down into two broad categories:

1. Strategic intelligence
2. Tactical intelligence

Strategic intelligence is concerned with gaining an understanding of a competitor's goals and strategy. Its goal is to develop the information necessary to predict your competitors' future moves, and how those moves might affect your company's competitiveness over the course of several years. It typically includes business level intelligence about your competitors, including:

- Target markets and positioning
- Major customers
- Suppliers and partners
- Intellectual property
- Product and portfolio roadmaps

Tactical intelligence, on the other hand, is not so concerned with being predictive but rather is focused on the information needed to ensure that you win in the market today. The focus is on data and analysis to improve shorter-term decisions in order to grow near-term market share and profit. Tactical competitive intelligence typically focuses on your competitors' product-level information such as:

- Positioning
- Competitive advantages
- Competitive issues
- Product specifications and architecture

- Current customers
- Positions they take against you
- Pricing

Your competitive intelligence acquisition efforts need to encompass both future-oriented strategic intelligence and here-and-now oriented tactical intelligence as seen in figure 41.

Strategic Intelligence	**Tactical Intelligence**
Future Business Level	Now Product Level

Figure 41: Strategic vs. Tactical Intelligence

Where to Find Your Competitive Intelligence

You'll be surprised at how many places you can find competitive intelligence. It's a little like walking through the woods. Wildlife is all around you, but if you're not looking for something specific, you'll never find it. Here are just some of the places that you'll find competitive information:

- Presentations by executive management that provide information about future strategies of the company.
- Annual reports and SEC filings.
- Articles, news stories, and other features created by someone inside or outside the company.
- Product specification sheets and other company literature distributed at conferences, trade shows, and other events.
- Physical observation of competitor activities at your customer sites, tradeshows, or investor events. For example, if you are in your customer's facility, keep an eye out for signs of a competitor's presence, like new equipment moving in, a worried

group of repair technicians gathered around an inoperative system, or business cards on your customer's desk.

- Special studies, research papers, and analyst reports about an industry and/or company.
- Networking with customers, suppliers, and other industry participants.
- Industry-specific social network sites.

No single source is likely to produce all of the competitive intelligence that you're looking for. Instead, you'll pick up tidbits of information from many sources that you'll need to assemble into a comprehensive profile for each competitor.

Who Does What

Collecting and analyzing competitive intelligence isn't going to happen on its own. An effective competitive intelligence system requires three primary activities:

1. Collect
2. Analyze
3. Disseminate

Tactical intelligence doesn't typically pop up in published materials. It is best found in close proximity to where your competitors and customers conduct their business. Therefore, it's the job of the field organizations like sales, applications, and service to be the primary collection points because they are closest to the information.

Strategic intelligence collection, however, is usually shared between the factory and field organizations, with the factory conducting the secondary research (annual reports, conference proceedings) and the field conducting the primary research (networking with customers, observing the competition).

The analysis process to turn raw competitor data into true competitive intelligence belongs to the factory, usually owned by the marketing and product management functions. It's their job to figure out what the data means to your business, reconcile conflicting data, and figure out how to respond.

Finally, for the competitive intelligence to be useful, it has to get into the hands of the people in your organization who need it. All of the collected intelligence and analysis needs to be packaged into a useful form and then disseminated to all of the key stakeholders. Strategic intelligence goes to management for business strategy development. Tactical intelligence needs to get back out to the field teams so that they can plan their next move and keep winning orders. The responsibility for disseminating competitive intelligence falls squarely on the factory marketing and product management functions. See figure 42.

Competitive Intelligence Activity	Responsibility
Collect	Tactical: Field Strategic: Factory, Field
Analyze	Factory
Disseminate	Factory

Figure 42: Competitive Intelligence Activities and Responsibilities

The System

The competitive intelligence acquisition system is a closed-loop management and control mechanism that ensures a rigorous, dependable process. It provides the structure to define the data that you need to collect and analyze. It establishes a routine to regularly assess gaps against the target intelligence, collects data to fill those gaps, and then updates your analysis and disseminates it. This process also inserts a regular inspection point to ensure that the system is working. See figure 43.

Before embarking on any competitive intelligence update mission, you'll need a framework to identify the specific information needed. The competitive intelligence system begins by creating two sets of templates, one for strategic intelligence and one for tactical intelligence. See the three-slide template in figure 44 for one way to organize your basic tactical intelligence.

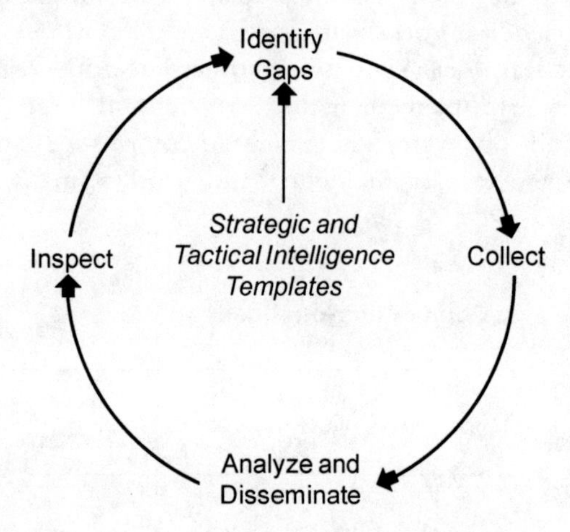

Figure 43: Competitive Intelligence Acquisition System

To get your system started:

1. Create the fill-in-the-blank templates that identify all of the competitive intelligence items that you need collected and analyzed. It's helpful to structure these in presentation format. That way when it comes time to disseminate and communicate it, your materials are ready to go without additional work.
2. Fill in all of the blanks in your new templates with the data that you already have.

Now you are ready to enter the closed-loop portion of the process. Your first step is to identify gaps. This is pretty easy to do—the gaps are now the holes or outdated data in your templates.

With a clear list of the gaps, assign the responsible stakeholders to seek out the specific information to fill those gaps. This kind of targeted assignment to collect specific data works much better than a

"Competitor Product Name" Snapshot

Description
- Key Feature #1
- Key Feature #2
- Key Feature #3

Top Customers
- Customer #1
- Customer #2
- Customer #3

Product Picture

"Competitor Product Name" Key Specifications

	My Product	Competitor Product
Key Process Specifications		
Specification 1		
Specification 2		
Specification 3		
Specification n		
Cost of Ownership Specifications		
Specification 1		
Specification 2		
Specification 3		
Specification n		

"Competitor Product Name" Position & Issues

Value Proposition and Positioning	Competitive Advantages
Competitive Issues	

Figure 44: Three-Slide Template for Capturing Tactical Competitive Intelligence

general request to the field such as, "Send in all of the information you have on the competition." The targeted approach sets a specific goal and challenge. Your team will be much more motivated with a clear objective and clear sense of what to do.

When the data comes in, it's time to aggregate and analyze it. You'll have to reconcile conflicting data points, perhaps validate certain inputs, and then update your templates. Disseminate the fresh competitive intelligence to all of your stakeholders. This is a really important step. Nothing will frustrate your field team more than to turn in the data and have it go into the proverbial black hole. Send the composite analysis to stakeholders and thank the team for their help.

Next is the regular inspection. This step is necessary because competitive intelligence acquisition has no natural deadlines in the course of conducting day-to-day business. If you don't do it, you'll still make the quarter's numbers, shipments still go out on time, and payroll still gets paid. But as you know, nothing ensures that a project will get done better than a highly visible deadline. Therefore, you have to manufacture a deadline for competitive intelligence acquisition within your company's management systems. Try including a competitive intelligence review as a regular, required feature in one or more of these forums:

1. Product-line reviews
2. Strategy reviews
3. Sales meetings

Provided that the forum occurs on a regular basis, it will serve as a constant reminder to maintain your competitive intelligence.

How to Plug the Tough Holes

Even with a robust competitive intelligence system in place, you're still going to have some tough holes to fill. Very often those holes have to do with specific competitor product details. For example, these may be details that you need in order to fully build out your value proposition or ensure that your positioning is effective.

One way to close those gaps is to go to the market with your best assumptions about your competition, and then let the market help you make corrections along the way.

Take the set of sales presentations that you already use to articulate your advantages and value proposition. This will be your starting point. Make sure that these presentations are very specific about how you are different from the competition. Instead of going "vague" in places where you don't have sufficient data about your competitor, stay very specific, but use your best guess to describe your competitor's capability.

For example, if you were trying to draw a distinction between you and your competitor on the cost of consumable parts, don't fall back to qualitative comparisons like:

"Lowest consumables cost"

Instead use your actual costs and your best guess for your competitor:

"Less than $150K/year in consumables versus $225K/year for our competitor"

Next, gather up those sales materials and get on the road. Present them to your customers, suppliers, prospects, and other industry participants, and you'll find that they will help validate or correct your assertions about the competition.

When you present "Less than $150K/year in consumables versus $225K/year for our competitor," at some point on your road trip, someone is going to correct you and say, "The competitor's consumables only costs $175K/year."

Bingo! You have your data.

Obviously, this process needs to be handled very carefully. Your approach will vary depending on the norms and culture of your industry. Be thorough enough to achieve your objective, but without compromising important industry relationships or anyone's integrity.

7. When and How to Execute Product Demonstrations

Capital equipment buyers, especially first time buyers, usually require a product demonstration before they commit to buy. The extent of the demonstration depends a lot on your reputation as a supplier and your customer's purchasing practices. At one end of the spectrum, a customer may only request to review demonstration data without witnessing the demo. At the other extreme, a customer may ask you to conduct an extended multi-day test simulating a real production environment with a full contingent of witnesses to observe the demo and analyze the data.

Whatever the specific situation, demonstrations are very risky. Too much can go wrong. The equipment could have an unexpected failure, the demonstration could expose a product weakness, or a member of the demonstration team could inadvertently do something to harm your position. In fact, demonstrations are so risky that the best salespeople actually aim to close orders without them.

However, no matter how hard you try, you are not going to forever escape the need to conduct successful demonstrations. That success will be born out of knowing when to use the product demonstration in the sales process plus careful planning and preparation.

When to Use a Demo in the Sales Cycle

Product demonstrations are best used to confirm a decision, not make one. By the time you bring a customer into the demo center to test drive your system, he needs to have already been convinced to buy. That means he's accepted your:

1. Framing of the important selection criteria
2. Value proposition
3. Advantages vs. the competition
4. Data and proof statements

The purpose of the demonstration is for the customer to get that final confirmation that everything you've been saying is true. So the right place for the demonstration in the sales process is right at the transition from "Create Value" to "Propose" stage as shown in figure 45.

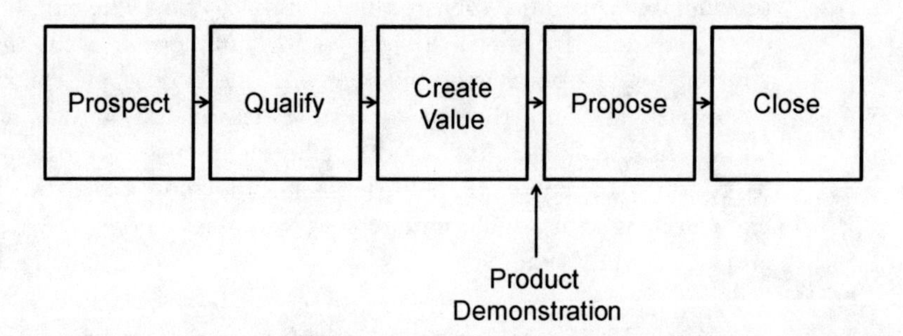

Figure 45: Best Time in the Sales Cycle to Use Product Demonstrations

One of the biggest mistakes that you can make is to use a demonstration before you have fully qualified customers. First, a demo at this premature stage just doesn't help advance the sales process. You're simply not far enough along for a potential buyer to act on the results of a demonstration. Sufficient details regarding purchase timing, budget, the application, and competitive position have not been developed well enough to define and execute a demo that will put you on a path to a purchase order.

Second, capital equipment demos are very expensive. The equipment can cost more than $1 million, it takes a team to prepare the system and execute the demo, and often the test materials are expensive. It's worth it when your demo-to-order close rate is high. But, that's not the case if you're demonstrating your equipment in the "qualify" stage of the sales cycle.

Probably the biggest abuse of the demonstration process is in the "Create Value" stage. It's pretty common to see attempts to jump straight from qualify to demonstration. This is a result of the false assumption that demonstrations can establish your value. They cannot. If you bring a customer in for a demo and you haven't moved your customer to a point where he has already made up his mind to buy from you, your demonstration will turn into a "prove your specifications" exercise. When this happens, your customer will take all of the demonstration data, lay it side-by-side with your competitors' data, and make up his own mind how to evaluate and weigh the results. That's not what you want.

So hold off on scheduling that demo until your customer is fully qualified, you've established your value, and all that is needed is a final proof point to confirm a decision that your customer is already prepared to make.

How to Prepare

The likelihood of success for a system demonstration is determined long before the customer arrives at your factory. It is all about how well you have prepared. Everything from the customer's expectations to the demo system itself must be in perfect order to assure a successful outcome. The preparation for a system demonstration follows these four steps:

1. Negotiate the demo plan
2. Conduct a demonstration plan and account situation review
3. Dry-run the customer visit and demo

4. Prepare the facility

Negotiating the demo plan is the most critical step. You don't want to be running open loop and allow the customer to run just anything that strikes his fancy. You'll want to run a demonstration that confirms your advantages against the competition. If you've been effective establishing value up to this point, the good news is that this will also be pretty well aligned to what your customer wants to do. A demo plan should be captured in a formal document that at least includes:

- What tests will be run, in what order, and how many times.
- Which tests will be witnessed live and which will just require a data review.
- The configuration of the system for the demonstration.
- What data will be collected and how.
- The definition of success.
- How the results will be analyzed and evaluated to determine if success was achieved.

Once the demo plan has been agreed to by both parties, it's time to conduct a full demo plan and account situation review with the team that will be hosting the customer and conducting the demo.

The account situation review is critical to avoid having anyone on the factory demo team inadvertently saying or doing something that could put the order at risk. This should be conducted by the account manager for the factory demo team and include:

- Current sales situation.
- Overview of what has been presented so far about system performance.
- Customer's view of your system's strengths and weaknesses.
- Customer's definition of success.
- Specific do's and don'ts for the demo team when interacting with the customer.

- Profile of each customer representative who will be attending the demo.

Then the demonstration plan itself should be reviewed with the entire demo cast. This should include:

- Top-level timeline review including preparation, practice run, execution, and results reporting.
- Full customer visit agenda that clearly identifies what is required for each agenda item and who is responsible for it.
- Demonstration system preparation plan including schedule, staffing, system maintenance, plus any logistics for securing spare parts or test equipment.
- Demonstration execution plan including test protocol, staffing, on-call technical support requirements, data collection, and contingency plans.

Just prior to the demo itself, you need to conduct a full practice run of both the actual demonstration and the non-demonstration elements of the customer visit. For the demo practice run, the demo team needs to execute the demo exactly as it will be run when the customer is present. That means the exact system protocol, same team, and same data collection methods.

For the balance of the customer visit agenda, agenda owners should review materials with the account team both to practice and to make sure that they are fully aligned to the sales objective.

The last step to get ready for the demonstration is facility preparation. This includes:

- Cleaning up demonstration room.
- Removing sensitive materials such as roadmaps and price books from areas that the visiting customer will access.
- Making sure that meeting rooms are reserved with projectors, clean white boards, and other necessary material.

Conducting a Successful Demo

If all of the planning steps were completed as described, conducting the demo itself will be easy. The demonstration starts the moment the customer walks in the door, and it doesn't end until the demo is complete and the customer is satisfied that all of the objectives have been met. Conducting a successful demo takes just three steps:

1. Review the plan
2. Conduct the demo
3. Follow up

The first step, reviewing the plan, is critical to make sure that everyone is still on the same page before the demo starts. You never know when your customer may have changed her mind, received a call from her boss with an additional request, or been prompted by a competitor to set a trap. So start every system demonstration with a review of the plan that includes:

- Tests that will be run
- How you will run them
- Data that will be collected and analyzed

Additionally, use this review meeting to address any issues or changes that have risen out of your practice run. If you need to modify, skip, or otherwise change a test protocol, now is the time to bring it up. Get the issue on the table right away; don't let the customer simply stumble onto it during the demonstration.

The second step is pretty straightforward; just conduct the demo according to your plan and compile the results in a demo report. Take time to produce a professional demo report and format it in a manner that is most useful to your customer. Your goal is to have the report submitted by your customer to his selection committee exactly as you have written it. If you are not sure how your customer needs the report written, just ask. Your customer will be happy to tell you what he needs if he can avoid rewriting the demo report.

The third step, the follow-up, is where you determine whether or not you have been successful, and this is the job of the account team. Once the demonstration is complete and all of the results have been reported, you need to formally review it with your customer and confirm that:

- Demonstration objectives have been met.
- Your value and advantages have been confirmed.
- No further demonstrations are required.

Once you have done this, you are ready to submit a formal proposal and start moving the sales process toward order closure.

Recovering from a Failure

We started this chapter emphasizing the high risk involved in executing capital equipment demonstrations. "High risk" means that sometimes demonstrations will fail, and you will find yourself scrambling to recover. If a demonstration failure occurs despite all of your planning, take these steps:

- Always provide the customer with a root cause analysis of the failure. This will showcase your company's disciplined approach to resolving issues and will give your customer an idea of what it will be like to work with you as a supplier.
- Try to negotiate a "do-over." If successful, rerun the test and update the demo report. Confirm that the revised data will be submitted by the customer to her selection team.
- Even if you cannot negotiate a "do-over," re-run the test and submit the updated results anyway. Even though you were denied, there's always a chance that she will change her mind and allow it to be submitted.

Remember, demonstrations are a high-risk, often very costly venture that you'd like to avoid. If you do have to conduct a demo, make sure that you insert it in the right place in the sales cycle, that you carefully plan every step, and that you are fully prepared to win.

8. Train the Sales Force to Win

It's the Monday morning senior staff meeting and there's some bad news. That big order that everyone was counting on still hangs in the balance.

The VP of Sales, on the speakerphone, tells the team, "The customer feels that anybody's system will work, so the decision is going to come down to price. We need to talk about how low we're willing to go."

The VP of Operations can't contain himself. He jumps up and jams the mute button.

"I've had it. Sales only knows how to compete on price, and they can't control the customer. Sometimes I'd swear they're on the customer's payroll, not ours."

But what if the mute button hadn't worked? The Sales VP may have had the following to say in his defense.

"I know that it sometimes doesn't seem like it, but I'd really rather compete on value. As a company, we're good at describing the technical genius that goes into designing our systems. However, we really need to show the customer how they will make more money buying our product instead of the competitions' product. I also need a value proposition that supports our pricing."

"Our customers are always raising objections to our product that I'm not sure how to address. And don't forget our competitors. Every day they suit up for battle with just one mission … to make sure that we don't accomplish ours."

The VP of Operations and the VP of Sales in our hypothetical exchange are actually both frustrated with the same thing. The sales force is not equipped to win.

You'll never fix this problem unless you take the time and make the investment to develop the necessary product skills in your sales force. This is separate from and shouldn't be confused with development of sales skills like negotiation, discovery, and organization mapping. Product skills equip the sales force to defend your pricing, address customer objections, and thwart attacks by your competitors.

This cannot be achieved through casual, hastily prepared, one-off sales training events. Product training for the sales force is critical to the capital equipment company's success, and to do it well, you'll need to:

- Make a commitment to continuous product skills development.
- Focus on solving the salesperson's biggest issues.
- Ensure learning through effective training delivery.

Commitment to Continuous Skills Development

You probably won't be successful knocking ten strokes off your handicap with just one golf lesson. When improving golf skills, the golf pro observes your swing, gives you a few pointers to correct key issues, and then has you practice what you've learned before you come back for your next lesson. Then, the cycle starts all over again. Each time through the cycle, your game gets a little better.

The same is true for improving sales force effectiveness. One product training session isn't going to suddenly cause a jump in market share and gross margin. Instead, just like in golf, improvement comes from continuous learning and practice. The most effective sales force product skills development programs follow a regular heartbeat of training events or sessions that build on each other to generate steady improvement.

One of the biggest challenges to establishing a routine for sales force product training is finding a lull in the day-to-day frenzy of making the quarter's numbers. Here's a tip. Try scheduling a quarterly sales training event the second week of every fiscal quarter. This is the time when you are most likely to catch the sales team's attention. They've just closed their quarter and so have their customers. With everybody busy counting the beans to figure out where they stand, the sales force has a moment to catch their breath. It's the perfect time to deliver your training.

This regular heartbeat of product training events also creates a recurring deadline for the marketing team, creating a recurring reminder to have their latest and greatest product positioning and selling tools ready for primetime.

Train to Solve the Biggest Sales Issues

If you ask your sales team what the biggest sales issues are, you can be pretty sure that they won't say, "I haven't had a product update lately." Yet, all too often that's about all they get from a product training session.

You've probably been to these types of meetings where the product manager takes the microphone with his deck of seventy-five slides showing the latest data, customers, new developments, and product features. It's all relevant to the product line, but it's not all relevant to helping the salesperson compete and win. It leaves the poor salesperson struggling to find those few valuable nuggets of information in that overwhelming slide deck.

Instead, product training should be focused on the three most important things that a salesperson needs to know to defend the product in the market. They are:

1. Why the customer should buy it at your price
2. How to handle customer objections to the product
3. What to do when the competition attacks

If you want a rule of thumb, the above three topics should comprise 80–90 percent of every product training session with the remaining 10–20 percent for general product and company updates. Now instead of just transmitting random product information, you're training the sales force to win and handle their toughest issues.

To make sure that your training is on target, ask the sales force where they need help before you set an agenda. Ask them:

- What part of our value proposition and product positioning is the weakest?
- What are the top customer objections to buying our system?
- What are the most difficult competitor attacks to defend?

There's no better way to figure out what's really needed by the sales force than to ask them. By asking these three questions, you'll get the list of the most important product skills that your sales force needs to win. Create your sales training agenda around their answers.

If you haven't been training the sales force this way, be forewarned; it will be a little uncomfortable at first. A Tekcess International client said the following when I first proposed this approach to building a training agenda:

"We can't do that! Sales is going to raise all kinds of questions that we just are not ready to answer."

This client was exactly right. By definition, when you get your feedback from the sales team on their toughest issues, you won't be ready to address them right out of the box. If you could, then they wouldn't be the biggest issues.

Just because you don't have a ready answer, however, doesn't mean that you can ignore the issue. When the sales team answers your three questions, they are speaking to you as the customer speaks to them. They are telling you the things that are keeping them from closing orders at the prices that your company needs to achieve. These issues cannot be ignored, and as a sales and marketing team, you don't have an option other than to figure out how to address them.

If you don't have the answers, you need to start developing them. This "biggest issues" approach to sales product training almost guarantees to focus the team's efforts on solving your company's most significant sales issues. It will put you on the path to close the most critical gaps in your ability to defend your product in the market.

Preparing to Train

You're going to have a good deal of content development work to do and holes to plug in your product marketing arsenal before you're ready to train. It can be overwhelming figuring out how to approach it. If you get stuck, try a preparation sequence something like this:

1. Gather the toughest issues from the sales force.
2. If there are more issues than you can handle, prioritize and select the most important. Make sure that you involve the sales force in this step.
3. Create an agenda around the selected issues.
4. For each agenda item, make a list of what you need to know in order to fulfill it. These lists will most likely be gaps in data and analysis for both your product and your competitors' products.
5. Identify the information on the lists that you don't have.
6. Assign owners and due dates to provide the missing information.
7. Turn the information into training and selling tools that will address the issues on the sales training agenda.

You can see that preparing for effective sales training is a lot of work, but it's very important work. Expect to invest significant time getting ready for a training event. It is not unusual to launch your first "what are your biggest issues?" survey to the sales team months ahead of a training session.

Rules for Delivering an Effective Training Session

You know a bad training session when you see one. Nobody's paying attention. The sales team's laptops are open to e-mail or stock listings. Cell phones are going off. The product manager at the front of the room has been there for two hours pointing to slides that only those with the best seats can read. And, you can hear the murmur of half a dozen side conversations.

All of the training preparation in the world won't impact sales success without effective training delivery. Your sales training sessions need to be highly interactive with everyone engaged. They also need to make sure that the sales team is ready to use their new skills the moment they get back in the field. Here are some rules for making that happen.

1. Practice-run the training.

   Getting the sales team to a central location for training is expensive, so you don't want to waste time once you have their attention. Get all of your materials and audio visual equipment debugged before the sales team arrives.

2. Use a facilitator.

   Managing a meeting of unruly salespeople and executives is hard. It's even harder if you don't have a facilitator to make sure that the training agenda is well designed and that the training event goes according to plan. The facilitator has two primary roles. The first is to design the training flow and learning activities. The second is to facilitate the training session to ensure continuity and provide for a productive learning environment in which the participants will feel safe participating and practicing new skills.

3. Set and enforce ground rules.

   If you want people to behave in a certain way during the sales training, you'll need to establish ground rules. An example set of ground rules might be:

- Cell phones off
- Computers closed (unless needed for training exercise)
- Return from breaks on-time
- One meeting, no side discussions
- Everyone participates
- Individual and out-of-scope issues will be addressed off-line

Get your ground rules on the table in the opening moments of your training session and keep them posted somewhere in the room.

Also, be prepared to enforce them. Penalty systems work well, like having to donate a dollar for every infraction.

4. Create a team competition.

Salespeople are competitive by nature, and they work best when "winning" is at stake. So design your training around a contest. For example, set it up so that every learning exercise such as a test or role play is an opportunity to earn contest points and even small prizes like team shirts or cash.

It's best to divide the participants up into teams. Team contests work best because peer pressure prevents anyone from disengaging from the training activities.

5. Emphasize dialogue, not monologue.

Nothing is worse than two days of listening to product manager after product manager give presentations. Instead, design your meeting with structured discussions and interactive application scenarios, role plays, and brainstorming exercises sprinkled into the training.

This also ensures two-way learning between trainers and trainees.

6. Slot in frequent learning checks.

To ensure that everything you are transmitting is being received, make sure that you slot in frequent learning checks along the way. This can include short quizzes, contests, role plays, or other methods to reinforce lessons learned.

Try to insert an interactive learning check for every forty-five minutes of new material in your training. It could be something as simple as dividing the group into small teams and asking them to take five minutes to jot down 3–5 things they learned that will help them sell.

7. Use the element of surprise.

   One of the best ways to keep everyone's attention is to be a little unpredictable. You can randomize how you select participants in learning exercises or insert a pop quiz that wasn't on the agenda.

   When your trainees see you use this technique once, they'll pay more attention. Nobody wants to be seen as unprepared.

8. Keep them moving.

   Don't make your trainees sit in chairs for hours on end. It's uncomfortable and will lead to fatigue. Instead, find ways to get them to move around, but try to be more creative than the "group stretch." For example, with a team exercise that requires work on a flip chart, have them get up and move to flip charts that are set up around the room.

9. Give plenty of breaks.

   Your trainees have a lot more going on in their lives than your training session. Respect that by providing plenty of breaks to check voicemail, call customers, and check e-mail. This will also put you on sure footing when you try to enforce your ground rule of returning from breaks on time.

10. Don't allow "sit-ins."

It's inevitable that some non-sales-related members of your organization are going to ask if it's okay to "sit in" on the sales training.

Your polite response should be, "This training is designed specifically to improve a salesperson's skills. If you would like for us to provide a separate session appropriate for your team, we'd be happy to do that."

"What's the harm?" you may ask? The harm is that these "sit-ins" will be a distraction. Since they won't be participating directly, they are very likely to test your ground rules. It's almost guaranteed that the first cell phone or side conversation violation will come from a "sit-in."

If they do participate, it's even worse. They will pull you off your main mission. The supply chain manager's question may be a great one, but it's unlikely to be critical to the salesperson's training.

11. Assign pre-work.

    To make the best use of your live training sessions, assign pre-work such as reading materials or preparing account profiles. So that everyone feels the pre-work was time well spent, integrate it into your live training session with a quiz or an interactive exercise based on it.

12. Evaluate the training.

    You want to ensure that the sales team is walking away with information and tools that make them more effective in closing deals. To do that, you need a mechanism, such as a survey, to get their feedback on what areas provided value, what areas need improvement, and what topics are a priority for the next training event. This is part of the continuous improvement process.

13. Reinforce the training.

> To cement the key concepts in the mind of the participants, you should consider sending out a brief meeting summary 5–10 days after the meeting that reinforces the key learning points and actions from the training. Also, try periodically reinforcing the major concepts from the training using on-demand social media like webcasts, podcasts, vlogs, or blogs.

In order for your sales force to be effective, you must equip them to defend your pricing, address customer objections, and handle attacks by your competitors. A commitment to product-skills development focused on solving the salesperson's biggest issues, delivered via effective training techniques, will put you on the road to developing a winning sales team.

9. Get off the Sales-Support Treadmill

One of the biggest killers of a marketing team's effectiveness is getting stuck on the sales-support treadmill. This happens when the majority of the marketing team's time is consumed with direct, tactical sales support instead of with the real marketing work of defining winning products and positioning them to win.

Ask the marketing organization why they don't spend time marketing, and you might hear:

"We don't have time because we are always doing sales support."

Or, is it the other way around?

Maybe they're always doing sales support because they haven't done the real marketing work. To fix this situation, you have to start with an understanding of the difference between marketing and sales, then recognize the symptoms of being stuck on the sales-support treadmill, identify what causes it, and, finally, decide how to get off of it.

The Difference between Marketing and Sales

Many people mistakenly think that sales and marketing are the same. As a result, they don't even recognize when their marketing team is stuck on the sales-support treadmill. The two functions are different, but they are both necessary for long-term success of the capital equipment enterprise. The most succinct way to describe the difference between marketing and sales is:

- Marketing creates demand.
- Sales creates transactions.

Marketing is everything that you do to create demand for your product. This encompasses defining products that will win as well as positioning their value and advantages in the market. Without marketing, you would not have products to sell or prospects to sell them too. To do their job, the marketing team:

- Identifies unmet needs in the market.
- Defines products that will satisfy market requirements and beat the competition.
- Establishes the product's position in the market.
- Creates and deploys selling tools.

Selling on the other hand, is the process of turning demand into an order. Without sales, you would not be able to convert prospects into customers. To do their job the salesperson:

- Creates and builds relationships with the prospect.
- Creates value in the mind of the customers by communicating your product's value as it applies to the prospect's point of view.
- Closes the sale.

The roles of marketing and sales are indeed different. Success requires that both jobs be done well.

Stuck on the Treadmill Symptoms

Just as sniffles and a cough indicate the onset of a cold, there are also clear symptoms that indicate that a marketing function is stuck on the sales-support treadmill. The symptoms include:

- Nearly all their customer visits are for tactical sales support.
- Specification responses can only be completed by the product expert.
- Every product presentation is a custom creation for a specific customer.
- The best presentations are still on their hard drives.
- Sales constantly calls with questions about the standard product.

Ask your marketing managers to think about the last time they spent days on a presentation, demo, or specification response to help one salesperson close one deal. Now contrast that to the time spent developing programs to create demand across your entire target market. They're stuck on the sales-support treadmill if they spend the majority of their time driving a single customer to adopt your solution rather than the whole market.

Root Cause

When none of the marketing infrastructure is in place, a salesperson will always drag in the product expert to directly support the selling effort. If demand hasn't been properly established and the selling tools haven't been developed, he has no choice. The root cause of a marketing function being stuck on the sales-support treadmill is that the marketing work has not been done.

Now imagine if …

- Your product and position were well established in the market.
- Your sales materials articulated a compelling value proposition with multiple levels of material, data, and case studies to prove it.

- Your sales materials addressed all of the key questions, objections, and issues that customers raise in the sales process.
- Your product specification answered 90 percent of line items in a customer's request for quotation.
- Access to those sales presentations and support materials were easy for the salesperson.
- You had a robust and continuous sales force product training program.

If the above were true in your organization, you can bet that the level of tactical support the sales team required from the marketing team would fall dramatically. To step off the sales-support treadmill, you must get your marketing infrastructure in place.

Getting Off the Treadmill

If at this point you've determined that your marketing team is in fact stuck on the treadmill, don't reach for that emergency stop button.

The marketing team has made itself a critical part of the order-closing machine. If you stop supporting sales cold turkey, orders could come to a grinding halt. Fixing this situation will require a gradual shift from sales support to true marketing. To do this, the marketing team will need to follow these three steps:

1. Determine which sales support activity is creating the biggest time sink.
2. Fix it.
3. Go back to number 1.

These projects might include developing specification documents, presentations, training programs, and quoting tools. Include anything that would enable the sales force to get the support that they need without pulling product experts directly into the process.

At first, the marketing team will struggle to find the time to work on these structural improvements. But each time they go through the three steps, they'll gradually reduce their time on the sales-support treadmill and thereby create more time for programs that will generate demand from the whole market.

Since the "urgent" has a tendency to overwhelm the "important," you are going to need a management and control system that ensures the marketing team is steadily weaning itself off the sales-support treadmill.

For example, if you had a routine of quarterly sales training events, you could use these events as deadlines for each incremental improvement in your marketing infrastructure. You could then build a continuous improvement process around this deadline like the one shown in figure 46.

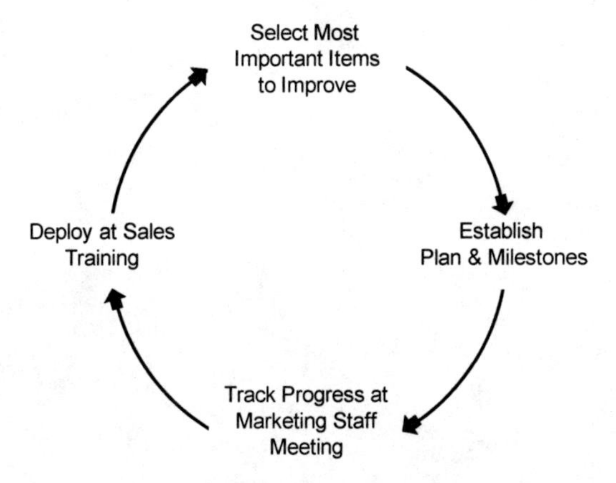

Figure 46: System for Continuous Marketing Infrastructure Improvement

Why it's Important

Really good high-tech marketing managers are hard to find. These folks are often a rare combination of product expert, strategist, leader, and communicator. When you have a good one, you want to get as much leverage as you can from her talents.

There's no denying that directly applying the company's premier product expert to a sales opportunity will help that one situation. But if every order requires this top gun to directly touch each step along the way, your total sales will be limited by her bandwidth. It's just not a scalable model.

You'll get much more leverage from your top marketing talent when she is creating the strategies, products, and infrastructure that will capture sales from across the entire market.

About the Author

Michael Chase is a twenty year veteran of the high-tech capital equipment industry. He has held executive-level positions in general management, marketing, and customer service in large and small capital equipment companies. In 2006, Mike formed Tekcess International, a consulting firm, to help high-tech capital equipment companies grow and compete.

Over Mike's career, he has assembled a track record of improving market share and profitability. He has developed and introduced multiple new products, driven corporate strategy, trained sales organizations, introduced disruptive technologies, broken into new markets, defined and implemented product strategies, and developed successful organizations.

Mike also publishes *The High-Tech Exec*, a monthly management newsletter for high-tech capital equipment executives. To learn more about Mike, Tekcess International, and *The High-Tech Exec*, please go to www.tekcess.com.

Get More Strategies, Tactics, and Tools

The High-Tech Exec is a free monthly newsletter published by Tekcess International and Michael Chase that tackles key issues facing today's high-tech capital equipment executive.

Readers get fresh perspectives and practical advice on capital equipment strategy, product management, and marketing.

To subscribe and see what your high-tech capital equipment colleagues are reading, go to www.tekcess.com.

Notes

Part I: Chapter 2

[i] Michael E. McGrath, "Product Strategy for High Technology Companies—Second Edition." (New York, McGraw-Hill, 2001), p. 3, 12.

Part I: Chapter 8

[ii] Michael E. McGrath, "Product Strategy for High Technology Companies—Second Edition." (New York, McGraw-Hill, 2001), p. 53.

LaVergne, TN USA
13 December 2010
208581LV00014B/6/P